Wild Mammals

A field guide and introduction
to the mammals of Zimbabwe

Dale Kenmuir
and
Russell Wi

Longman Zimbabwe

Longman Zimbabwe (Pvt) Ltd
Tourle Road, Ardbennie, Harare

Associated companies, branches and representatives throughout the world

First published 1975
Ninth impression 1994

ISBN 0 582 64164 0

The Publishers' policy is to use paper manufactured from sustainable forests

Printed in Zimbabwe by National Printing and Packaging, Harare

Contents

Dale Kenmuir, a biologist, wrote the text for this book; Russel Williams, a game ranger, did the illustrations.

Both are former employees of the Department of National Parks and Wildlife Management of Zimbabwe.

The Bundu Series of books has been derived from the earlier series published with the aid and help of the Standing Conference of National Voluntary Youth Organisations in Zimbabwe.

Acknowledgements

A great many people helped us during the preparation of this book. We should like to thank the following, in particular, for very kindly assisting us in numerous ways: the Ossie Bristow family, Errol Button, Mike Coke, Dr John Hanks, Mr B. L. Mitchell, Sid and Shirley Robbins, and Mrs A. G. Williams.

In addition, we should like to acknowledge the help, at various times and in various ways, of the following:

J. Anderson
G. W. Begg
G. Bell-Cross
Mrs R. Black
D. K. Blake
B. Brien
Dr G. Child
Dr T. Choate
B. Couper
M. Drury
J. H. Grobler
D. Hughes
H. D. Jackson
H. Jordaan
Dr M. Keep
Dr A. Kemp
Mr and Mrs N. S. Kenmuir
M. A. Kerr
Mr and Mrs K. Loubser
L. Magarangomah
Mr and Mrs D. F. McKinlay
W. T. Miller
G. Mills
Tim and Jill Paulet
P. H. Read
R. B. Rees
Dr H. Van Rompaey
D. Rowe-Rowe
R. d'Ivry Russell
John Russell
R. M. Smith
P. Steyn
J. Stutchbury
The late J. M. C. Uys
A. J. S. Weaving
V. J. Wilson
N. A. Wright
P. J. Wright

We are grateful to Professor G. Fortune and his assistants, Mr A. C. Hodza, Mr S. J. Mhlabi and Mr K. G. Mkanganwi, at the Faculty of Languages, University of Zimbabwe, for preparing the list of African names. We should also like to thank the Department of Information and the Zimbabwe National Tourist Board; the staff of the Queen Victoria Museum and the Department of National Parks and Wildlife Management for allowing us to make use of their library facilities; and the directors of the National Museums and Monuments of Zimbabwe, and the Durban Museum, for kindly permitting us to use their specimens for illustration purposes.

It would not have been possible to write this book without the wealth of written information about mammals which is available today. Our thanks are therefore due to the many individuals and organisations who have contributed, through their research efforts, to this fund of knowledge.

Introduction

This book aims at serving as a field guide to the larger mammals of Zimbabwe, as well as introducing the reader to the entire range of mammals to be found in Zimbabwe, from the smallest to the largest.

All too often the smaller mammals are left out of field guides simply because the author feels that, unless he or she can do full justice to the subject of smaller mammals, they should not be touched at all. The result is a paucity of information on all the smaller mammals, a proliferation of information on the larger mammals, and a great many people who know the difference between a kudu and an impala, but for the life of them couldn't tell you what a mole rat is, or looks like, or how it differs from a golden mole, or what a dormouse is, and how it differs from an ordinary mouse, or what an elephant shrew looks like, and so on.

Hopefully, this book will help the reader to become slightly more familiar with the smaller members of the mammal community, and possibly whet his or her appetite for the more detailed studies on the subject which will undoubtedly appear in future years. With the aid of this book the reader should have no trouble in identifying, as far as the family level, any smaller mammal found or seen. Although there are sixty species of bats, for example, these can be easily grouped into several different families, and any bat found can quite easily be identified according to its family grouping. The same is true of other small mammals. *All* mammals found in Zimbabwe have been mentioned, together with their common and scientific names (from Smithers, 1973; Smithers and Wilson, 1979), and therefore this book should be useful as a source of reference as well as for identification purposes.

With regard to the larger mammals, from the hedgehog upwards, the combination of colour illustrations and black-line drawings should assist the reader in identifying a species in the field by bringing out salient features as well as the colour of the animal in question. Written description has therefore been kept to a minimum, and only conspicuous features mentioned. For the benefit of the holidaymaker a list of the larger mammals that may be seen in Zimbabwe's many game parks and reserves has been provided (see Fig. 3 and accompanying table).

Illustrations of the spoor and droppings of the majority of large mammals have been included for those interested in tracking, hunting or simply identifying mammals in the field from *sign*. A word of warning, however. These drawings should be regarded rather as a guide than as a dogmatic assertion. Droppings of a single species can vary tremendously from area to area, depending on the diet of the animal at that time of the year, its size, condition and so on. Similarly, spoor can differ depending on the substrate it was made on, the size of the animal, thc speed at which it was moving, and so on. Nevertbeless, the majority of these drawings and the measurements were made in the field and as such they are reliable representations of the originals drawn.

The mass (weight) of a species can also vary from area to area, and the figure given in the drawings is merely an indication of the mass of the species, and should not be taken as an exact figure.

With regard to distribution of a species within Zimbabwe, this refers, unless otherwise stated, to the natural distribution, and not distribution as modified by artificial introductions of the species to various game reserves.

The section *Points to ponder* has been included to encourage the reader to think of mammals in terms of the environment and the habitat in which they live rather than simply as isolated objects to be viewed from an indifferent distance in an unthinking way. Animals should be thought about and not simply looked at, and, for those with a deeper interest in mammals, perhaps this section will start the cogs rolling and the mind questioning, and make game viewing an absorbing pastime.

Vernacular names

Where there are two entries for the Shona name, the one to the left of the oblique line is that found in the Zezuru dialect, the other is that of the Karanga dialect. Where there are two entries for the Ndebele name, one is simply an alternative for the other and either name may be used.

Points to ponder

What is a mammal?

A typical mammal can be described as an animal that has a backbone, warm blood, breathes air, suckles its young on milk from the mother's mammary glands, has a four-chambered heart, regulates its body temperature by a mechanism in the brain, and maintains this temperature by body hair.

How and why are mammals classified?

Mammals are classified into three major groups. The first group contains the MONOTREMES, which are primitive animals that lay eggs, such as the well-known duck-billed platypus. The second group contains the MARSUPIALS, whose offspring are born prematurely developed and complete their development attached to a nipple, usually in the mother's pouch; this group is exemplified by the kangaroo. The third group is the largest, containing the PLACENTAL mammals. In this group the young are nourished by a placenta in the mother's body, and are born at an advanced stage of development. The placental mammals are classified into seventeen major groups, or ORDERS.

The question of classification puzzles many people. Why are animals classified or placed in such and such a group? The answer is very simple. If an animal is completely unlike any other animal, if it is *unique*, it is placed in an ORDER entirely of its own, and not put handily in with some other group. The antbear is a good example: it is unlike any other animal, has no obvious affinities with any other animal (that is, it has no relatives), and thus it is placed in an ORDER entirely of its own. It is the only member, the only species, of the ORDER Tubulidentata.

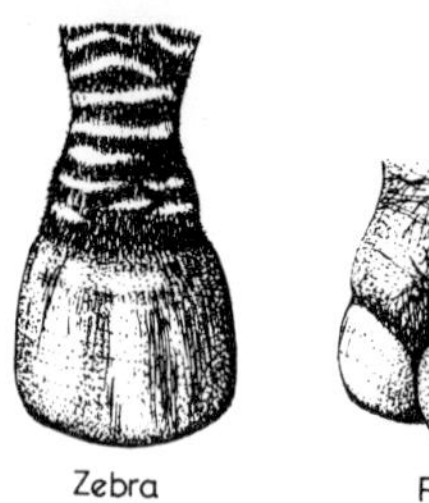

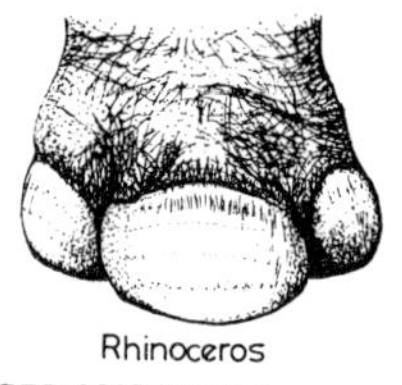

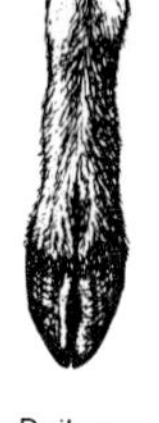

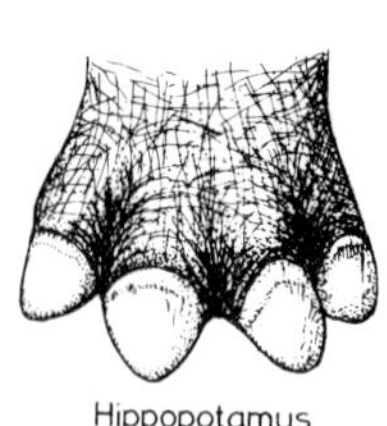

Fig. 1

When animals have certain features in common, and quite obviously so, they are placed in one group. The animals with hooves, for example, have one noticeable feature in common — they all have hooves. They are placed loosely together in a group known as the UNGULATES (which means, literally, hoofed animals). This is one of the bases of classifying mammals — FEATURES IN COMMON (usually morphological features). Once the main group has been established, further breakdowns take place. Of the hoofed mammals, for example, some have an even number of toes (cloven-hooved), while others have an odd number of toes (horses, zebras, rhinos). These ungulates are split into two major groups (see Fig. 1), the PERISSODACTYLS (meaning odd-toed) and the ARTIODACTYLS (meaning even-toed). Each group is then divided again into different categories according to certain features. All the artiodactyls which chew the cud, for example, are placed in a group called the RUMINANTIA (ruminants; having complex stomachs, like a buffalo), while those that have simple stomachs and do not chew the cud are called SUIFORMES (wild pigs, hippo), and then again, all the ruminants which have unbranched horns growing around a bony core are placed in a group called the BOVIDAE. This group includes the antelope, the sheep and goats, and the cattle-like animals. And so one continues to break each group down into separate groups, until the lowest levels of classification are reached. The lowest categories are the GENUS, the SPECIES, and the SUB-SPECIES.

Behind the scenes classification is more complicated, and a classifier or taxonomist must have an expert knowledge of the anatomy, physiology and history of animals in order to be able to classify them properly. No single factor can be used as a comparative criterion for classifying mammals. If mammals were classified only according to the structure of their teeth, for example, one might find the dassie and rhinoceros in the same group, as their cheek teeth are very similar; or further afield, the manatee would find itself in a group with the sloths. Many factors must be taken into account before it can be decided that one animal is or is not related to another. Take the mole rat and the golden mole, for example. By virtue of the fact that the animals are about the same size and both burrow underground, one might be tempted to think they were related and should be in the same group. How wrong one would be! An expert would go further into the comparison and would study not only their mode of life, but also their morphology. He would study their teeth, for example, and find that the two animals have completely different teeth. The golden mole has teeth adapted for an insect eating diet, while the mole rat has teeth adapted for a vegetarian diet of tubers and rhizomes. In effect, he would find that the golden mole has INSECTIVORAN teeth, while the mole rat has typical RODENT teeth. One is an insectivore, the other a rodent.

The point here about classification is that although two animals may lead almost identical lives, and may look very similar (a phenomenon known as CONVERGENT EVOLUTION), they may not be related in any way, and may belong to entirely different groups. The taxonomist must delve into their structure and evolutionary history to classify them correctly.

On the other hand, animals may lead very different lives and yet, because of structural similarities and evolutionary affinities, be related (DIVERGENT EVOLUTION). Who would imagine, for example, that the dassie is distantly related to the elephant?

Over the centuries, animals have adapted to their environment through a process of natural selection, gradually changing to meet the demands of the physical and social worlds, until the fantastic diversity of species that we find today, with different shapes, sizes and ways of life, was arrived at. But, nevertheless, underlying all these differences are basic similarities which the taxonomist digs up and uses to categorise animals. Naturally there are still many unsolved mysteries. Nobody really knows, for example, what group of animals the pangolin evolved from — as the textbooks say, 'Its relationships are obscure'. So for the moment, or forever, the pangolins dwell in splendid isolation in an ORDER of their own.

There are many points of disagreement between taxonomists, and no two taxonomists are ever likely to produce exactly the same classification. Some place the aardwolf, for example, in a family separate from that of the hyenas, while others place them together. Thus any classification is of a rather arbitrary nature, and likely to depend as much on the author's point of view as it does on the latest findings of taxonomic research.

The most important classification groups

The major classification groups are the: KINGDOM, PHYLUM, CLASS, ORDER, FAMILY, GENUS, SPECIES.

For example, we would classify a bushbuck thus:

KINGDOM:	*Animalia* (animals, as opposed to plants)
PHYLUM:	*Chordata* (animals with a notochord or primitive backbone at some time in their development)
CLASS:	*Mammalia* (mammals, as defined earlier on)
ORDER:	*Artiodactyla* (even-toed hoofed mammals)
FAMILY:	*Bovidae* (with unbranched horns, from a bony core)
GENUS:	*Tragelaphus* (the bushbuck, kudu, nyala group)
SPECIES:	*Tragelaphus scriptus* (bushbuck)

Within each group further breakdowns would take place. For example, one could have included a sub-order, Ruminantia, or a sub-family, Tragelaphinae. As bushbuck vary tremendously in colour from one area to another, one could have included a sub-species category, for example *Tragelaphus scriptus ornatus*. Most people are not interested in detailed classification however, and for the purpose of this book a simple breakdown into order, family, sub-family (in the antelope only), genus and species has sufficed.

Structure and function

When looking at mammals in a game park one should not simply just look and say, 'Ah yes, that's a waterbuck.' One should delve further into the subject and say, 'Ah yes, that's a waterbuck. Now let's see, why has he got a white ring on his backside?' Well, why has he? Your theory may be as good as the next man's, or better.

I am trying to make two points here. The first is that animals have features, peculiarities, STRUCTURES, for special reasons. They are adaptations for the animal's particular habitat and way of life, and they perform some FUNCTION or other. Horns, for example, are STRUCTURES, and their FUNCTION is defence.

Nothing better illustrates the point of structure and function than do the teeth of an animal. The structure of their teeth is directly related to their diet (the function of eating). Their structure may be adapted for gnawing, as in the rodents, for killing, cutting and chewing, as in the carnivores, for cropping grass and then macerating it, as in the hooved mammals, or for catching hold of and crunching up insects, as in the insectivores. Amongst other things, mammals are classified according to their teeth, and a mammal may be identified from the skull by examining the teeth. Examples of the skulls and teeth of the different orders of Zimbabwean mammals are shown in Figs 5a and 5b.

In considering structure and function one should also remember that the same structure on different animals does not always serve the same function, and here again nothing serves better to illustrate this point than that structure at the other end of the animal's body, the tail. A tail (see Fig. 2) may be used for swishing flies away, for balance, for support, for warmth, for protection, for propulsion, for steering, for sending alarm signals, and even for clinging to branches. It may even be used in more way than one. Whatever the case, the structure, or nature, of it will be related to its function. And where there is no necessity for a tail it is either absent or reduced.

Fig. 2

The second point that I wanted to make was that the interpretation or reason, the answer as to why the animal has such a feature, either of anatomy or behaviour, is not only the realm of the scientist, but can also be the realm of the interested and enquiring layman. Why, for example, does the hippo wag its tail when it defaecates, spreading its dung all over the place? There are various theories as to why and how this habit originated, and your theory may be as feasible as any other. One theory is that dung scattering is used as a way of marking out an animal's territory. Why does the bushbuck have spots and stripes, and why does the white rhino have a hump?

Many questions are posed when one looks enquiringly at game, and one should not be afraid to try to find intelligent answers for the questions.

The distribution of species

The question of structure and function, or adaptation, also brings in the question of the *distribution* of species. Obviously, where an animal is adapted to a particular habitat, it will be found only in that habitat, and hence its distribution will be related to the distribution of its preferred habitat. The klipspringer is a good example. With its short blunt cylindrical hooves it is adapted for life on steep and rocky hill-sides, and its distribution is therefore confined to areas where such a habitat occurs. The springhare, by virtue of the fact that it needs sandy soil in which to dig its burrows, will not be found in areas where the substrate is extremely rocky. Vervet monkeys, adapted for climbing, and requiring trees in their habitat for survival purposes, will not be found in areas where there are no trees.

Thus the distribution of species is influenced largely by habitat requirements.

Man plays an important part in altering the natural distribution of the species. Habitats, otherwise eminently suitable for a species, may be unoccupied because of the threatening presence of man. Eland, for example, were at one time extremely numerous on the present site of Salisbury. They no longer occur there, not because the habitat is unsuitable, but because man has driven them out.

Man can also alter the distribution pattern, not by driving a species out, but by bringing it in. This has happened widely in recent years, where areas, hitherto with small or restricted game populations, have been declared game reserves, and new species brought in from elsewhere. Such exercises are called *translocations*, and are part of general game management policy.

Possibly the most famous translocations of all time are those involving white rhino, over one thousand of which were transported from Natal to various parts of the world. Of this number, over ninety were sent to Zimbabwe where they were introduced to Hwange, Victoria Falls, Kyle, Matopos, and McIlwaine.

In Zimbabwe, the first translocations took place in the late 1950s, when over-population was becoming apparent in the southern part of the Hwange National Park. The newly fenced game parks in McIlwaine, the Matopos and Kyle were stocked with giraffe, zebra, and a number of antelope species, brought from Hwange.

Since those days a great many more internal translocations have taken place. Up to 1966 over seven hundred animals involving twenty-seven species were introduced to Kyle, McIlwaine and the Matopos parks. While most of the animals involved were antelope, including nyala from Natal, other species included a pangolin, a number of jackals, and three aardwolves.

Other major translocations in recent years, some of which have received considerable publicity, have been the removal of black rhino from Kariba to Kruger National Park, from areas in the north of Zimbabwe to Gona-re-Zhou, and from the Binga-Sengwa area to Hwange. Lichtenstein's hartebeest have been taken from the Gorongoza area of Mozambique to Gona-re-Zhou, and roan antelope have gone to Kruger from Tsholotsho. A unique exercise was the removal of hippo from pools drying up in the Lundi to other dams and pools.

It stands to reason that these introductions and translocations rather alter the distribution of species. If the introduction of a species to a game reserve is particularly successful the species in question will probably extend its range outside the boundaries of the park to areas where it was hitherto absent, particularly if it is a small species, and hence a new distribution pattern comes into existence. Thus, to a certain extent, the distribution of mammal species in Zimbabwe cannot be considered static or permanent but rather in a state of flux, subject to change brought about by man's activities.

One further point: an essential *prerequisite* for the successful introduction of a species to a new area is a thorough knowledge of the animal's likes and dislikes, its preferred habitat, its habits, and in fact everything there is to know about it. There is no sense in introducing a grass-loving species like the tsessebe to an area with wooded hill slopes, or a species like the kudu, which favours wooded hill slopes, to an open grassy region. Knowledge of the animal's way of life beforehand will prevent such mistakes being made.

This is why a great deal of wild life research is taking place today. It is unfortunate, but true, that the survival of many species today depends on them being moved from an area where they are threatened to an area where they can live in peace.

Game spotting by sign

Trying to interpret what animals are present in an area when you *can't see them* is a fascinating and absorbing pastime. Studying SIGN is an age-old game usually practised by the hunter, but for the layman it can be a rewarding pursuit and may serve some practical purpose (you may be a farmer, for example, trying to determine what animal has been robbing your chicken run).

Animals leave numerous signs behind them. SPOOR is the most obvious thing to look for. With a good knowledge of spoor, an intelligent layman can rapidly narrow down the field of possibles when studying it. Take that cat spoor in the chicken run. Was it really a cat? Have a good look — there are claw marks. Cats (with the exception of the cheetah) don't leave claw marks, so rule out cats. What small carnivore does have claws? Civets, honey badgers and jackals all leave claw marks. Is the spoor typically dog-like? No — so rule out jackals. Could it be mongoose or genet? The spoor is too big for them — so rule them out. So now the field has been narrowed down considerably and you have a very good idea of what *might* be raiding your poultry run. DROPPINGS or SCATS are also indicators of what animals are around. While walking in the bush, suppose you find a great pile of droppings in which there are the remains of chongololos and insects, bits of fur and bone, and wild fruit pips. If you do not immediately know the answer, first ask yourself, what carnivore always defaecates in the same place (that is, a midden), and secondly, what carnivore has a very varied diet (eating things like chongololos, wild fruit, small mammals). Consult the literature or an expert, and you will find the answer — civet. Suppose you find some large buck droppings, and you break open a pellet and find the contents are bits of grass. Quite obviously, the buck in question is a grazer and not a browser. It could be a sable, but definitely not a kudu. Thus not only the *size*, *shape* and *contents* of the droppings tell a story, but also the *manner* in which they are left.

When trying to determine what animal is leaving sign around you should also consider what type of HABITAT you are in. This could give

Plate 1 Elephant shrew *Peter Steyn*

Plate 2 Hedgehog *A. J. S. Weaving*

Plate 3 Golden mole *W. T. Miller*

Plate 4 Night-ape *W. T. Miller*

Plate 5 Yellow-spotted dassie *Dale Kenmuir*

Plate 6 Cape pangolin *Dale Kenmuir*

Plate 7 Bush-baby *W. T. Miller*

Plate 8 Rock dassie *Dale Kenmuir*

Plate 9 Antbear *E. L. Button*

Plate 10 Fruit bat *John Visser*

Plate 11 Samango monkey *G. M. Brooks*

Plate 12 Insect eating bat *Russell Williams*

you a clue. If, while toiling up a rocky mountain in the Matopos, you come across a pile of buck droppings, the rocky habitat should lead you immediately to suspect klipspringer. If you are in broken woodland country and you find large buck droppings, you should immediately suspect kudu. Of if you find cat spoor in rank vlei near water, you should suspect serval which are often associated with water. Thus, a good knowledge of the type of habitat the animal *normally* lives in will help. A word of warning though: one cannot apply laws to game as there are always exceptions to disprove the rule, and many animals also have a wide habitat tolerance (the duiker, for example), so the habitat aspect is a guide, and not a definite indication.

There are many other signs to look for. What the animal has been *feeding* on will give you a clue as to what the animal is: berries plucked from bushes and scattered around wastefully, some eaten, others discarded — baboon; a half eaten impala stuck in the fork of a tree — leopard; a hole dug deep into an anthill — antbear; and so on. Then there are your VOCAL signs. The loud unmistakeable bark of a bushbuck, the chittering of an irate squirrel, the raucous call of the bushbaby, the shrill clamour of dassies, the rasping grunt of a leopard — these are all tell-tale sounds.

Other INCIDENTAL, but important, signs may be porcupine quills scattered about; or a hole worn smooth, perhaps with no cobwebs in the entrance, or with flies buzzing around it, indicating that it is being used.

Occasionally, or more often, depending where you reside, you may find bits of a skeleton in the bush (SKELETAL sign). The skull with teeth in is invaluable in determining what sort of animal you are dealing with. If the skull has horns, naturally it is a bovid, and the deceased animal can be identified from an illustration of antelope horns (see Figs 4a and 4b). If it is a small skull with well developed incisors and a gap between these and the cheek teeth, it is a rodent's skull — and so on.

This is all merely an introduction to veld lore. An expert can read a great deal from the bush. The satisfying thing about this subject is that one can never learn enough — there is always something just around the corner still waiting to be learned.

Reading sign is as satisfying as being able to successfully translate a foreign language into your own mother tongue.

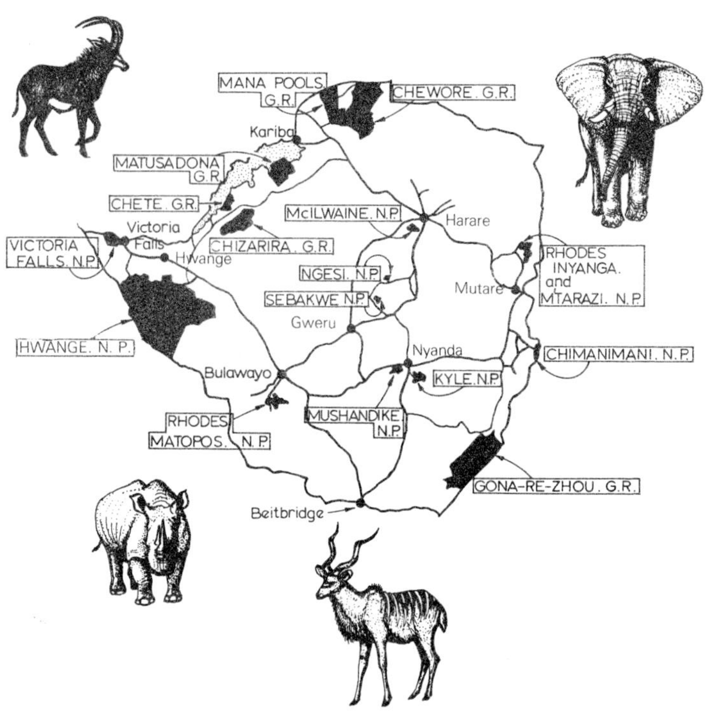

Fig. 3 Game reserves and national parks in Zimbabwe

	Hwange	Victoria Falls	Chete	Chizarira	Matusadona	Mana Pools	Chewore	Kariba	McIlwaine	Ngezi	Sebakwe	Mushandike	Kyle	Rhodes Matopos	Gona-re-Zhou	Chimanimani	Rhodes Inyanga
Elephant	●	●	●	●	●	●	●	●							●		
White rhino	●	●							●				●	●			
Black rhino	●	●	●	●	●	●	●	●							●		
Zebra	●	●	●	●	●	●	●	●	●	●	●		●	●	●		
Hippo	●	●	●		●	●	●	●		●	●	●	●	●	●		
Giraffe	●	●							●				●	●	●		
Buffalo	●	●	●	●	●	●	●	●					●	●	●		
Warthog	●	●	●	●	●	●	●	●	●	●	●	●	●	●	●		
Bushpig	●	●	●	●	●	●	●	●	●	●	●	●	●	●	●	●	●
Eland	●	●	●	●	●	●	●	●	●		●		●	●	●	●	
Roan	●	●	●	●	●	●	●							●	●		
Sable	●	●	●	●	●	●	●	●	●	●	●	●	●	●	●	●	
Gemsbok	●																
Wildebeest	●								●				●	●	●		
Red hartebeest	●																
Lichtenstein's hartebeest															●		
Tsessebe	●		●	●					●				●	●			
Waterbuck	●	●	●	●	●	●	●	●	●	●	●	●	●	●	●		●
Kudu	●	●	●	●	●	●	●	●	●	●	●	●	●	●	●	●	●
Nyala						●	●						●		●		
Bushbuck	●	●	●	●	●	●	●	●	●	●	●	●	●	●	●	●	●
Impala	●	●	●	●	●	●	●	●	●	●	●	●	●	●	●		
Reedbuck	●	●	●	●	●		●		●	●	●	●	●	●	●	●	●
Common duiker	●	●	●	●	●	●	●	●	●	●	●	●	●	●	●	●	●
Blue duiker																●	●
Oribi	●								●	●	●	●	●		●		
Grysbok	●	●	●	●	●	●	●	●	●	●	●	●	●	●	●		●
Steenbok	●	●							●	●	●	●	●	●	●		●
Suni			●			●									●		
Klipspringer	●	●	●	●	●	●	●	●	●	●	●	●	●	●	●	●	●
Lion	●	●	●	●	●	●	●	●							●		
Leopard	●	●	●	●	●	●	●	●	●	●	●	●	●	●	●	●	●
Cheetah	●	●	●	●		●		●						●	●		
Black-backed jackal	●	●					●		●	●	●	●	●	●	●		
Side-striped jackal	●	●	●	●	●	●	●	●	●	●	●	●	●	●	●	●	●
Bat-eared fox	●	●													●		
Samango monkey																●	●
Wild dog	●	●	●	●	●	●	●	●							●		
Spotted hyena	●	●	●	●	●	●	●	●					●	●	●		●
Brown hyena	●													●			
Caracal	●	●	●	●	●	●	●	●	●	●	●	●	●	●	●	●	●
Serval	●	●	●	●	●	●	●	●	●	●	●	●	●	●	●	●	●

Some mammals to be seen in the game reserves of Zimbabwe

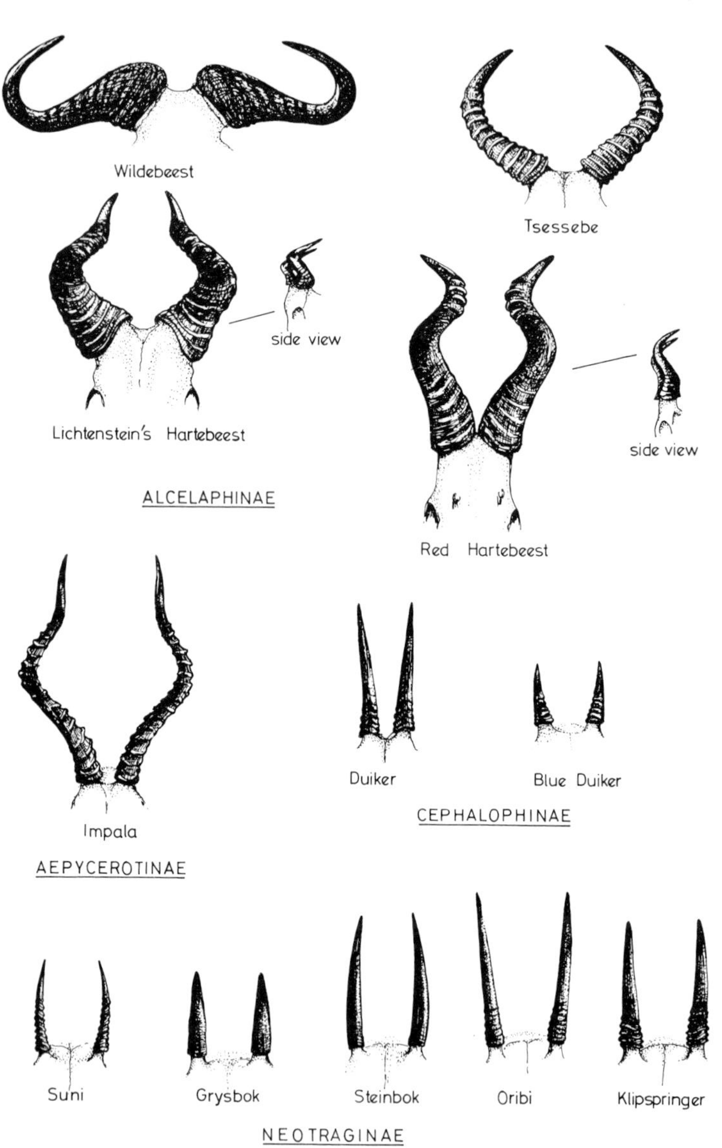

Fig. 4a Horns of the antelope

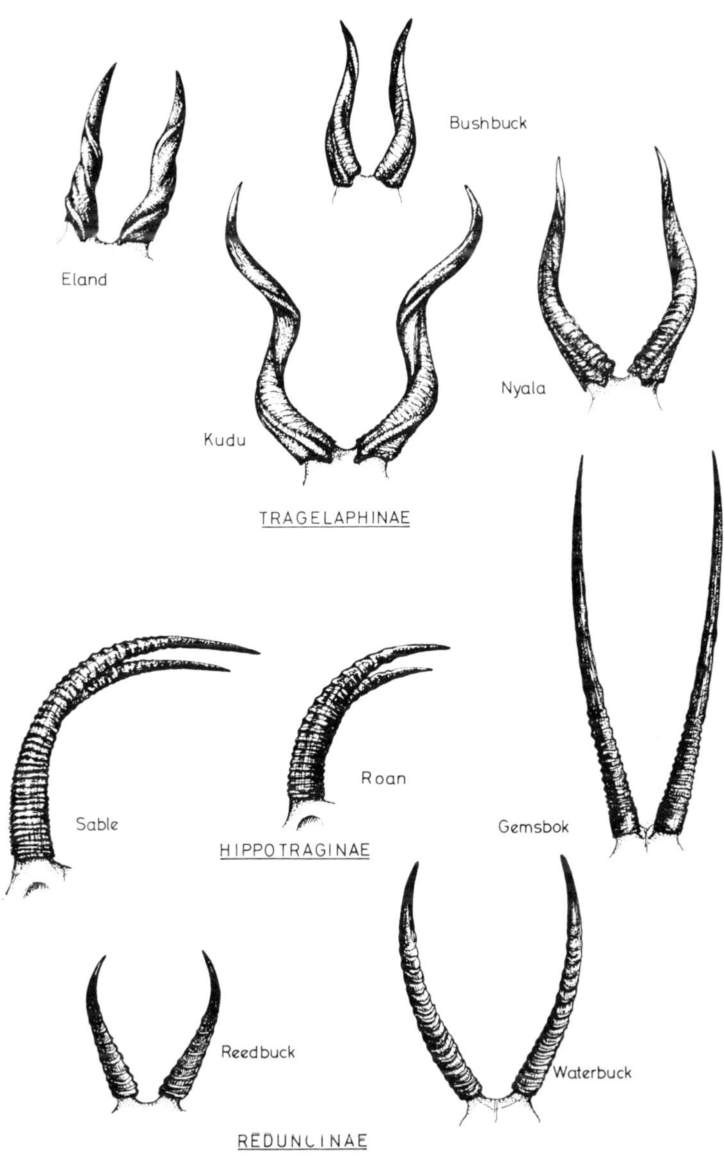

Fig. 4b Horns of the antelope

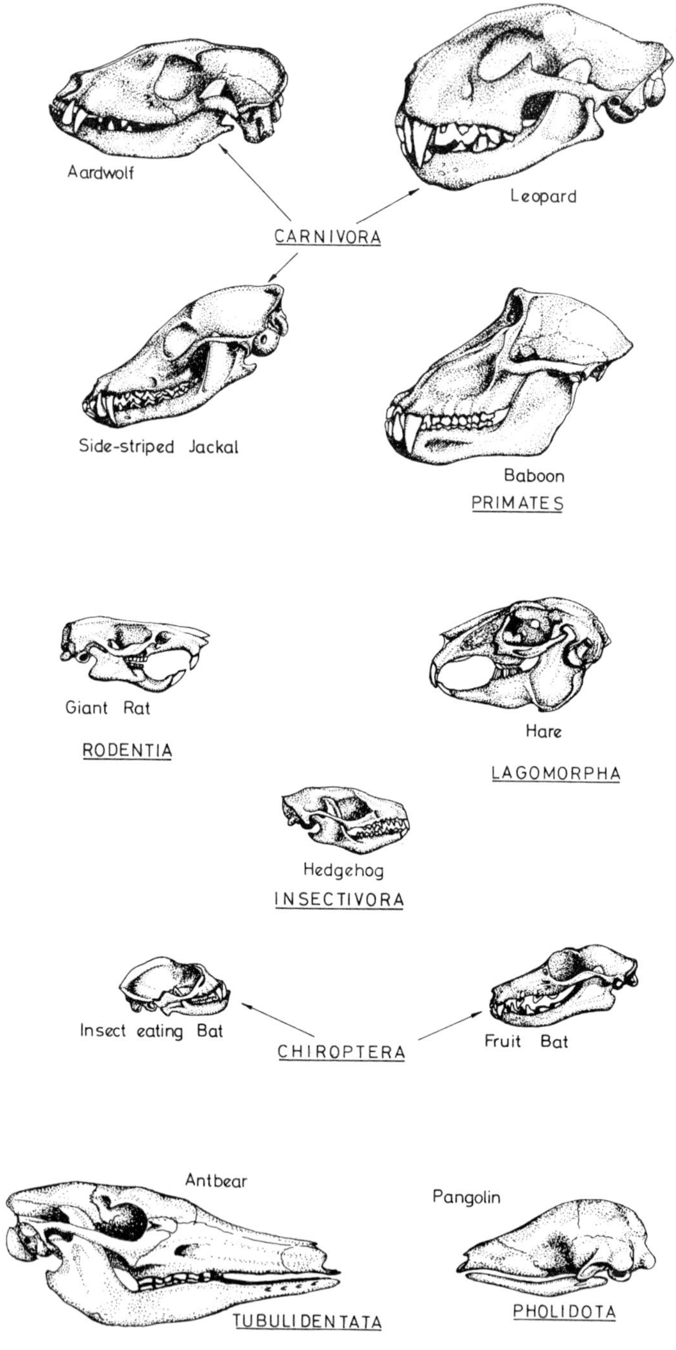
Aardwolf
Leopard
CARNIVORA
Side-striped Jackal
Baboon
PRIMATES
Giant Rat
RODENTIA
Hare
LAGOMORPHA
Hedgehog
INSECTIVORA
Insect eating Bat
CHIROPTERA
Fruit Bat
Antbear
Pangolin
TUBULIDENTATA
PHOLIDOTA

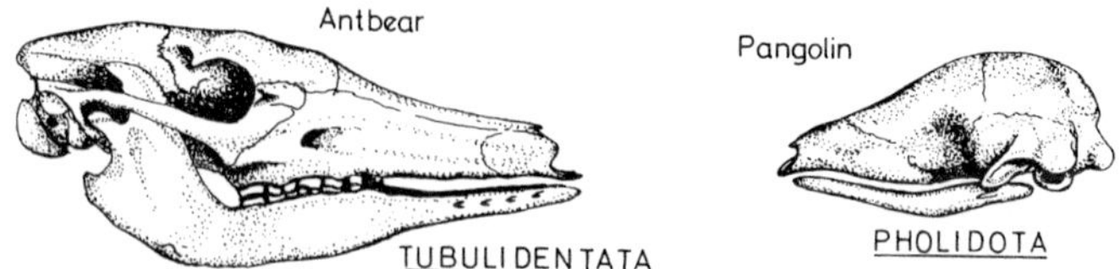

Fig. 5a Skulls of Zimbabwean mammals

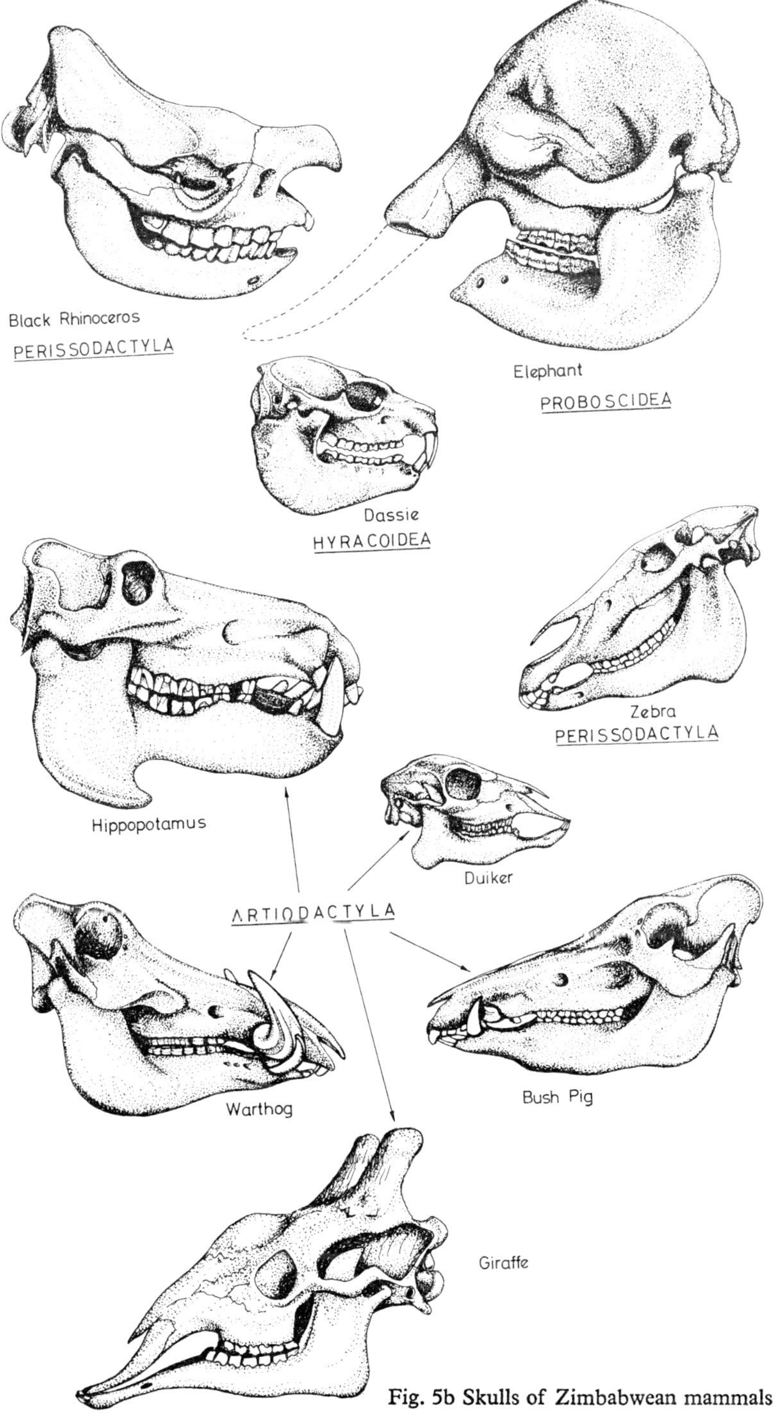

Fig. 5b Skulls of Zimbabwean mammals

Order Insectivora: insectivores

The insectivores are mainly nocturnal, and are small, primitive mammals that have remained virtually unchanged for millions of years. Scientists believe that the present day insectivores are little changed from the earliest mammals. They have small brains and eyes, teeth that are rather unspecialised, and fingers and toes that are clawed. They feed on a wide variety of invertebrate animals, such as worms, insects and molluscs, as well as smaller vertebrates. Well known members of this order are shrews, hedgehogs and moles.

Altogether there are eight families, making up a total of three hundred and seventy-four species, the vast majority of which are shrews. In Zimbabwe there are four families making up a total of seventeen species. More than half of these are shrews.

Fig. 6a

Fig. 6b

Family Soricidae: shrews

Shona: dune, mudhende/dhenge, muchuchu
Ndebele: untswebe

One very seldom sees shrews, since they are very small, secretive mammals (the world's smallest mammal is a shrew), and although diurnal to an extent, they are more active at night. Generally the only shrews one ever actually sees clearly are the ones brought in and discarded by the cat. They are not eaten by carnivores because of their unpalatable odour and taste.

Their distinguishing feature, apart from their small size, is the pointed snout which is flexible and very mobile. The eyes are small and thus it is the sense of smell which is most important in finding food. There are five toes to each foot and each has a small slightly curved claw (see Fig. 6a). They have a reputation for being voracious feeders and, in fact, eat a wide variety of invertebrate animals including insects, earthworms and molluscs as well as small vertebrates, either living or dead.

They are generally solitary and hide in holes, under brushwood, in heaps of rubbish or in any suitable protective cover. The young are born under cover and generally number from two to five.

Eleven species of shrew are known to occur in Zimbabwe. Seven of these are musk shrews (Crocidura spp.), while the remaining four are the greater and lesser dwarf shrew (*Suncus lixus*, *S. varilla*), the dark-footed forest shrew (*Myosorex cafer*), and the climbing shrew (*Sylvisorex megalura*).

The musk shrews are the giant (*C. flavescens*); reddish grey (*C. cyanea*); lesser red (*C. hirta*); katanga (*C. luna*); black (*C. mariquensis*); tiny (*C. bicolor*); maquassi (*C. maquassiensis*).

Family Macroscelididae: elephant shrews

Plate 1

These are interesting insectivores in that they have an extremely long and tapering snout which wiggles and twitches as it sniffs the air and is rather a fascinating sight. It is something like an elephant's trunk, hence the name elephant shrews (see Fig. 6a).

They are more or less intermediate in size between rats and mice but, whereas most of the latter are nocturnal, elephant shrews are mainly diurnal. Another characteristic of the elephant shrews is the elongated back legs with which they proceed in hops and leaps, rather like a miniature kangaroo. In fact they are also known as jumping shrews although they do also walk and run. Other noticeable features are the large eyes and ears and the fairly long tail.

Rock elephant shrews can often be spotted in a rocky habitat, like that found in the Matopos hills.

They feed largely on insects, termites and ants and they live in shallow burrows, holes, rock crevices, under logs or in the holes of termite mounds. One often detects their presence in an area without actually seeing them, by the small dark droppings which, when broken open, show the chitinous remains of insects.

There are three species in Zimbabwe — the short-snouted elephant shrew (*Elephantulus brachyrhynchus*), the rock elephant shrew (*E. myurus*) and the four toed elephant shrew (*Petrodromus tetradactylus*).

Family Chrysochloridae: golden moles

Shona: nhukutsa
Ndebele: umvukuzane (?)
Plate 3

Golden moles are entirely confined to Africa and take the place of the true moles of Eurasia. The majority of them occur in southern Africa. Superficially, they resemble true moles with features adapted for life underground. The eyes, for example, are only rudimentary and are hidden under the skin so that, in effect, the animal is totally blind. The ears are only minute cavities in the skin and the muzzle carries a hard pad which is used for turning up the soil. The limbs are very short; the fore feet are adapted for scraping out the soil and have four clawed toes, two of which are enormously enlarged; the hind foot carries five toes, all with sharp slightly curved claws. The fur of golden moles is thick and characteristically has a metallic golden to violet lustre (see Fig. 6b).

They burrow just beneath the surface of the earth, or deeper down, throwing up mounds of fresh earth at regular intervals. Their food consists mainly of worms, insect larvae and other animal matter. Golden moles differ from true moles in that the latter have no 'set' to the fur, which can lie in any direction so that the animal can move either forwards or backwards in its tunnel. The golden mole also differs in that its nails are of unequal length, one being greatly developed, whereas in the true moles the nails are more or less equal, giving the hand its spade-like appearance. There is also a difference in the articulation of the forelimbs.

There are twenty species altogether of which two occur in Zimbabwe: the yellow golden mole (*Calcochloris obtusirostris*) and Arends' golden mole (*Chlorotalpa arendsi*).

Family Erinaceidae: hedgehogs

Hedgehogs, of which there are fifteen species altogether, range throughout Europe, Asia and Africa. They are characterised by the fact that their upperparts are covered with short barbless spines (the true hedgehogs) or very rough harsh fur (the hairy hedgehogs). When disturbed they can roll into a ball for protection.

They are mainly nocturnal and feed on a variety of animal matter, including insects, worms, snails, young rodents and birds' eggs. Those living in cold climates hibernate during winter.

Zimbabwe has one species.

HEDGEHOG, *Erinaceus frontalis*
Shona: shoni
Ndebele: inhloni
Fig. 7 *Plate* 2

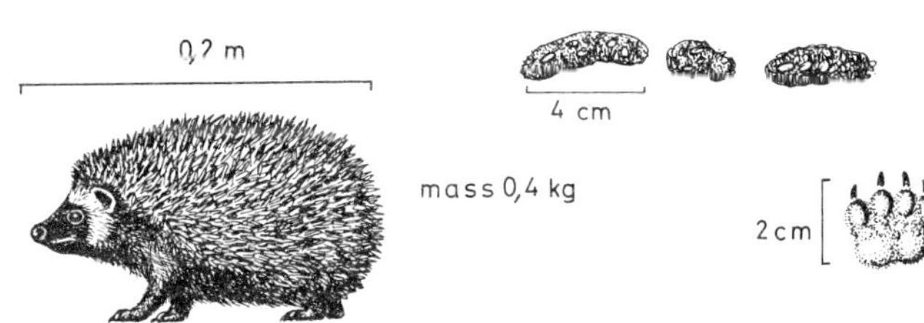

Fig. 7

Features Hedgehogs are well known little animals and need no description. Their most characteristic features are their prickly spines and their ability to roll themselves up into a ball to protect their soft underparts when molested. They have a distinct white band on the forehead.

Habits They are largely nocturnal, occur singly or in pairs (or in family groups of a mother with her young) and are omnivorous, eating a wide variety of invertebrate animals, including insects, termites, millipedes, centipedes, slugs and snails, as well as small vertebrates such as frogs, mice, lizards and even snakes, and also wild fruits and other vegetable matter.

Their sense of smell is very well developed and used extensively for locating and grubbing up food. The food is always well chewed up before it is swallowed.

During the day they hide in convenient piles of brushwood or rubbish, in thick undergrowth or litter, or in other suitable places. During the cold winter months hedgehogs are very inactive and are seldom encountered. Their distribution in Zimbabwe is localised and confined to the Midlands area west to the Bulawayo area.

Breeding The young, normally numbering up to six but occasionally more, are born about November in the sheltered places mentioned above. The gestation period is about forty days.

Distribution This species occurs only in southern Africa.

Order Chiroptera: bats

Shona: chiremwaremwa
Ndebele: ululwane

Bats are the only mammals with true powers of flight. There are almost one thousand species in the world, making them the second largest group of mammals, after the rodents. Zimbabwe alone has fifty-five species, comprising almost one third of the total mammal species (they are, in fact, the largest group found in Zimbabwe).

Bats are divided into two major groups, the fruit eating bats (Megachiroptera — one hundred and fifty species) and the insect eating bats (Microchiroptera — over eight hundred species). As can be seen, by far the larger number of bats are insect eaters. In Zimbabwe, for example, fifty-three bats out of sixty-eight are insect eaters.

Features Because of their peculiar way of life, bats have some interesting habits and characteristics. They are best known for their remarkable habit of navigating by echo-location. For this purpose, the bat emits from its large larynx very high pitched short-wave squeaks, inaudible to us, which bounce off objects and are picked up by the bat. The echoes thus received are analysed and interpreted and the bat manoeuvres accordingly. Thus, instead of being able to see objects in the dark the bat 'hears' them! This sense is most highly developed in the insect eating bats which often have elaborately developed and highly specialised ears. In complete darkness the normal bat can avoid a wire of less than half a millimetre in thickness. The pulse may be emitted either by the mouth or by the nose, depending on the species. Echo-location is a comparatively new concept for man but bats have been using it for at least fifty million years.

When a female bat gives birth she grips onto her perch with the claw of her thumb as well as with her hind feet, so that she is in a horizontal position. She then curves her tail so that the young one falls into the 'hammock' created by her body. At first the young is carried about, hanging to the underside of the mother's body by the milk teeth, which have specially backward directed hooks, and the claws of the hind feet. Later, as it gets bigger, the young bat is left behind.

When bats excrete they hang by their thumbs and thus avoid fouling themselves.

Bats, compared with other small mammals, have an incredible life-span. Whereas a small mouse may live for only a few years, a small bat will live comfortably for twenty. Scientists are studying the reasons for this unusual longevity.

The hind legs of bats are peculiar in that the knee flexesback wards instead of forwards as is usual in mammals, and the foot is also directed backwards and contains toes of equal length, each with hooked claws for hanging onto objects. The shape of bats' wings (thin membranes of skin) varies from species to species. In the swift fliers, they tend to be long and narrow, like those of the swiftest birds, whereas in the slow fliers, they are broad and rounded. Fig. 8 shows the main features of Zimbabwean bat families.

FRUIT EATING BATS

Fig. 8 *Plate* 10

Distribution These are mostly large bats, confined to the tropics of Asia, Africa, northern Australia and New Guinea. The largest bat in the world, the flying fox, with a wing span of one and a half metres, belongs to this group. There is only one family, Pteropodidae, containing all the species.

Features Characteristic features of fruit bats are the long fox-like snout, the simple ears, the presence of a claw on the second digit (absent in the insect eating bats), the tail which is only rudimentary or even absent, and the tail membrane which is incomplete or absent. The teeth are small or poorly developed (an adaptation for their fruit eating diet) and the eyes are larger than the other groups since sight is an important sense to them. Only one species, the Egyptian fruit bat, is known to have a sonar system (this species occurs in Zimbabwe). These bats also have an acute sense of smell which is used to locate food. Some fruit bats feed only on nectar, having long tongues and muzzles with which to do so.

Zimbabwean fruit bats The following species occur in Zimbabwe: the straw-coloured fruit bat (*Eidolon helvum*), a well known yellow-coloured fruit bat with a wide distribution in Africa, occurring from Senegal to Somaliland and south to the Cape, and which occurs in Zimbabwe only as a rather uncommon migrant; Bocage's fruit bat (*Rousettus angolensis*); the Egyptian fruit bat (*R. aegyptiacus*), with a wing span of three quarters of a metre and found in Asia Minor and widely in Africa, and three species of epauletted fruit bats; Wahlberg's epauletted fruit bat (*Epomophorus wahlbergi*); Peter's epauletted fruit bat (*E. crypturus*); and the Gambian fruit bat, a very uncommon species (*E. gambianus*). The epauletted fruit bats are so named because the males have a fold of skin on the shoulder which can be extruded to show a conspicuous tuft (epaulette) of white hairs. Dobson's fruit bat (*Epomops dobsoni*) is recorded only from the extreme north-west in riverine forest.

Wild fruits, including wild figs, the fruit of the ebony (Mushenje),

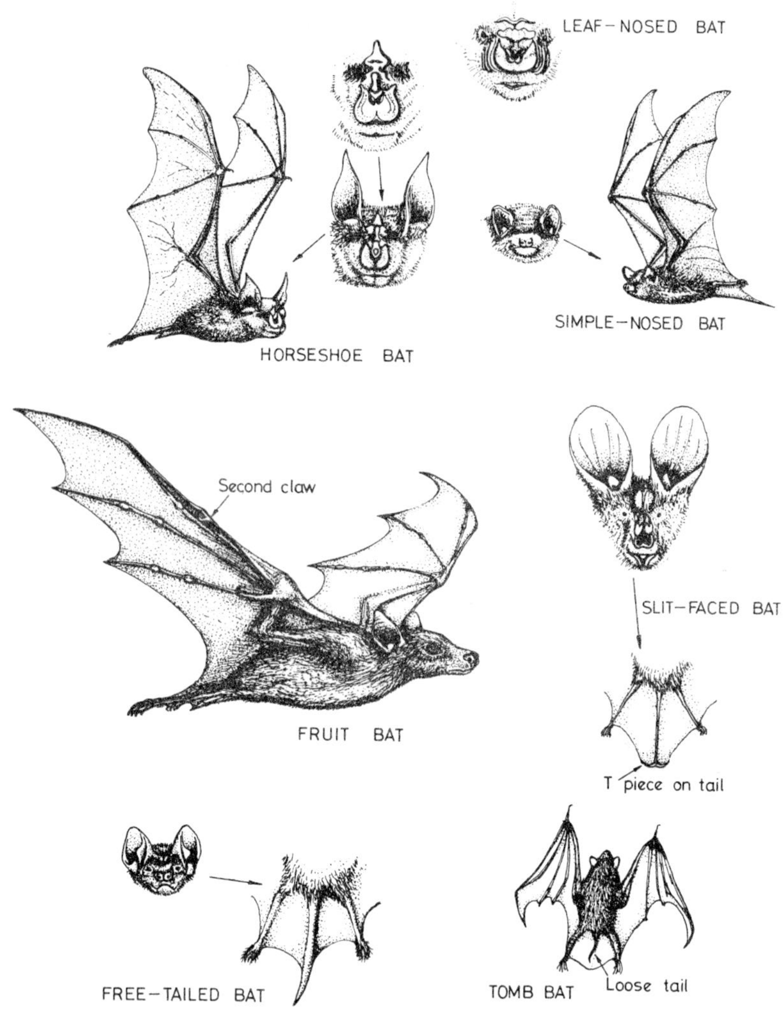

Fig. 8 Bat families with identification features

the mabola plum and marulas, as well as cultivated fruits, such as guavas, loquats, bananas, and so on, are eaten by fruit bats.

INSECT EATING BATS

Fig. 8 *Plate* 12

Distribution Unlike the fruit bats, which are confined to the tropics and subtropics, the insect eaters extend into the colder temperature regions, where they hibernate in winter. Some species have deviated from their diet of insects. Examples are the well known vampire bat, the fish eating bat, and the false vampires which are carnivorous.

Features They are mainly small bats, characterised by their large complicated ears (used in echo-location), well developed teeth (for eating insects), an index finger without a claw (the fruit bats have a claw) and a tail that is often long and usually enclosed in the membrane. Many of them have nose-leaves, which are elaborate skin folds used in echo-location.

Zimbabwean insect eating bats Zimbabwe has fifty-three species of insect eating bats, classified into six families (Fig.8). The following notes are intended primarily to assist the reader to identify a bat as far as the family level. However, the different species found in each family are also included for reference purposes.

Family Emballonuridae (Tomb bats, or sheath-tailed bats) These bats have a short tail free of skin, leathery ears and scantily haired bodies. The name, sheath-tailed, is derived from the fact that the tail projects above the membrane and fits loosely into the wrinkled skin, as if into a sheath. They are fast and skilful fliers. The two species are the Mauritian tomb bat (*Taphozous mauritianus*); and the Egyptian tomb bat (*T. perforatus*).

Family Nycteridae (Slit-faced, hollow-faced or long-eared bats) Characteristic features are the long loose fur and a groove, or slit, extending from the nostrils to between the eyes and ending in a pit in the forehead. Another interesting feature is that the tail has a T-shaped tip and the ears are large and oval. The five species are the hairy slit-faced bat (*Nycteris hispida*); the Egyptian (*N. thebaica*); the large (*N. grandis*); the large-eared (*N. macrotis*); and Wood's (*N. woodi*).

Family Rhinolophidae (Horseshoe bats) These bats have a very complex nose-leaf extending over the upper lip, round the nostrils, and coming to an erect point above their nostrils. The appendage rather resembles a horseshoe. The ears are large, widely separated, and pointed. The nine species are Geoffroy's horseshoe bat (*Rhinolophus clivosus*); Darling's (*R. darlingi*); Dent's (*R. denti*); Swinny's (*R. swinnyi*); bushveld (*R. simulator*); Lander's (*R. landeri*); peaksaddle (*R. blasii*); Rueppell's (*R. fumigatus*); and Hildebrandt's (*R. hildebrandti*).

Family Hipposideridae (Leaf-nosed bats) These bats are closely related to the horseshoe bats and also possess a nose-leaf. However the posterior leaf is rounded and not triangular in shape. Some authors include them with the horseshoe bats. They generally inhabit caves, mineshafts, and so on. The four species in Zimbabwe are Sundevall's leaf-nosed bat (*Hipposideros caffer*); Commerson's (*H. commersoni*); the trident bat (*Cleotis percivali*); and the Persian leaf-nosed (*Triaenops persicus*).

Family Molossidae (Free-tailed bats) In these bats the tail emerges from the middle of the posterior margin of the membrane between the back legs and extends well beyond it. Other features are the rounded ears, which are about as broad as they are high, and the thick wrinkled lips. They usually have narrow wings, velvety fur, and no nose-leaf. The twelve species in Zimbabwe are Martienssen's free-tailed bat (*Otomops martiensseni*); Robert's flat-headed bat (*Sauromys petrophilus*); Madagascar large (*Tadarida fulminans*); large-eared (*T.lobata*);Egyptian (*T. aegyptiaca*); Ansorge's (*T. ansorgei*); Nigerian (*T. nigeriae*); little (*T. pumila*); Angola (*T. condylura*); Midas (*T. midas*); spotted (*T. bivittata*); long-crested (*T. chapini*)

Family Vespertilionidae (Simple-nosed bats, vesper bats) This is a very large family, composed of the typical insect eating bats. Some of the other families are probably specialised offshoots of this family. They are very small bats with tiny eyes, generally without a nose-leaf, and with long tails which are included in the interfemoral membrane or with the last joint free. This is the largest family in Zimbabwe. The species are the rufous mouse-eared bat (*Myotis bocagei*); the Cape hairy bat (*M. tricolor*); Welwitsch's bat (*M. welwitschii*); Cape serotine (*Eptesicus capensis*); long-tailed serotine (*E. hottentotus*); the banana bat (*Pipistrellus nanus*); the rusty bat (*P. rusticus*); Kuhl's bat (*P. kuhli*); Rueppell's bat (*P. rueppelli*); the butterfly bat (*Glauconycteris variegata*); Schlieffen's bat (*Nycticeius schlieffeni*); the giant yellow house bat (*Scotophilus gigas*); the yellow house bat (*S. nigrita*); the lesser yellow house bat (*S. leucogaster*); Schreiber's long-fingered bat (*Miniopterus schreibersi*); the greater long-fingered bat (*M. inflatus*); lesser long-fingered (*M. fraterculus*); the Damara woolly bat (*Kerivoula argentata*); Harrison's woolly bat (*K. harrisoni*); Botswana long-eared bat (*Laephotis botswanae*); and Aloe serotine bat (*Eptesicus zuluensis*).

Plate 13 Vervet monkey *A. J. S. Weaving*

Plate 14 Chacma baboon *H. Van Rompaey*

Plate 15 Black-backed jackal *A. J. S. Weaving*

Plate 16 Bat-eared fox *Dale Kenmuir*

Plate 17 Striped polecat *W. T. Miller*

Plate 18 Side-striped jackal *Dale Kenmuir*

Plate 19 Wild dog *Dale Kenmuir*

Plate 20 Honey badger *Dale Kenmuir*

Plate 21 Spotted hyaena *A. J. S. Weaving*

Plate 22 Brown hyaena *Gus Mills*

Plate 23 Aardwolf *W. T. Miller*

Order Primates: primates

This is the order to which man belongs. One of the most important features of members of this order is a large brain which has given them a high degree of intelligence. Primates are adapted primarily for an active arboreal existence and their hands and feet are able to grasp branches (having an opposable thumb) while their forward directed eyes allow them to judge distances when moving about in trees. Sight and hearing, rather than scent, are their most important senses. Another feature of primates is that the digits have flat nails instead of claws.

Primates are divided into two groups: the prosimians, which include the less advanced primates (lemurs, bush-babies, lorises and tarsiers) and the anthropoids, which include the more advanced primates (monkeys, apes and man). Anthropoids have better developed brains and generally have flatter and more expressive faces than the prosimians. Most of them are diurnal, whereas many prosimians are nocturnal.

Altogether, there are one hundred and ninety-three species of primates in the world, the majority occurring in Malagasy, Africa and southern Asia, and the remainder in South and Central America. Zimbabwe has rather a paucity of species, containing only five representatives of this order (Uganda for example has about seventeen species, a reflection of a greater diversity of habitats). The bush-baby and night-ape represent the prosimian group and the vervet monkey, samango monkey and the chacma baboon represent the anthropoid group. The primates, like other orders, are divided into a number of families.

Family Galagidae: galagos

These are less advanced primates, being smaller, with pointed snouts, sharp teeth and a clawed second hind toe which serves as a fur comb. They are nocturnal and arboreal and are found in the warmer regions of the Old World, being particularly common in Malagasy.

There are eleven species, three of which occur in Zimbabwe.

BUSH-BABY, *Galago crassicaudatus*
Shona: chinhavira/chidavira
Ndebele: impukunyoni
Other names: thick-tailed bush-baby, greater galago
Fig. 9(1) *Plate* 7

Features This is the largest of all the galagos. It may be recognised by the thick woolly coat, the long bushy tail (slightly longer than the body) and the very thin membranous ears which are also convoluted. Like the night-ape, the second toe of the hind foot is different from the others and adapted for grooming fur (see Fig. 9a below).

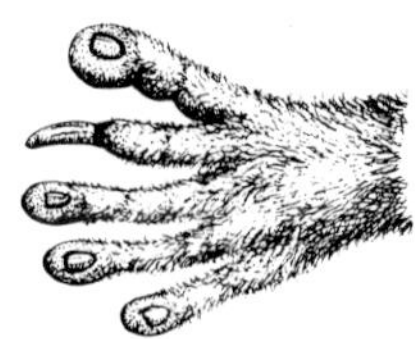

Fig. 9a

Habits Bush-babies are not as widely distributed in Zimbabwe as are the smaller night-apes, and are more common in central and eastern Zimbabwe, where they inhabit woodlands, plantations and forests, than in the drier western parts of the country. They are nocturnal, solitary and arboreal, although they do descend to the ground and are also gregarious at times. They move along branches silently and nimbly and, like night-apes, are capable of making prodigious leaps. Their presence in an area is usually indicated by their raucous screams at night, often repeated several times over a short period. These calls probably serve to advertise their territory.

They have a very omnivorous diet, feeding on fruit, berries, seeds, leaves, flowers, gum, insects and smaller vertebrates such as birds and lizards and birds' eggs. They are also known to kill poultry. They are easy to keep and feed in captivity, but can be treacherous.

Breeding The young are born in secluded places from about August to November. Normally two young are born but in other parts of Africa three have been recorded.

Distribution They are mainly confined to the southern part of the continent, although they extend north up the east coast of Africa to Somalia. Owing to their larger size and greater dependence on thicker bush, they are not as common or as widespread as the night-ape.

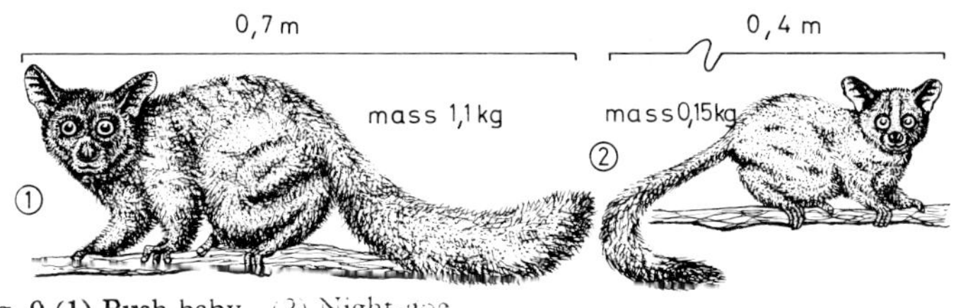

Fig. 9 (1) Bush baby (2) Night-ape

NIGHT-APE, *Galago senegalensis*
Shona: chinhavira/chidavira
Ndebele: impukunyoni
Other names: nagapie, lesser galago, Senegal galago
Fig. 9(2) *Plate* 4

Features Night-apes are very much smaller than bush-babies and also very much more agile. They have attractive and alert little faces in which the eyes and ears are very prominent. The hind legs are long and adapted for leaping, and they have softly furred bodies and long furred tails. Their eyes are often picked up in car headlights. The second toe of the hind foot is different from the others and adapted for grooming the fur.

Habits Night-apes are nocturnal and occur singly or in pairs. One can often see them in the early evening as they leave their holes in tree trunks to move out to their feeding grounds. They have regular routes along the trees, and a fairly large gap between trees is no deterrent to them as they have prodigious powers of leaping (a vertical leap of seven metres or more is commonplace). They are widespread throughout Zimbabwe but are most common in Acacia and Mopani woodlands where the many holes in the trees are probably important requirements for their lives, as they provide nesting sites. In built up areas they often have their little leaf-lined nests in the roofs of houses.

Their diet is varied and, although consisting mainly of insects (beetles, caterpillars, moths and so on), it also includes wild fruits, berries, tree gum, flowers and possibly small vertebrates. Night-apes are easy to keep and feed in captivity. Large owls are their main enemies.

Breeding Up to three young, although mostly two, are born in the nests towards the end of the year. When distressed, the young utter shrill cricket-like squeaks which are undoubtedly audible to their parents from a good distance.

Distribution This species is the most widely distributed of the African galagos, occurring in bush and savanna country both north and south of the equator.

Family Cercopithecidae: monkeys, baboons

This primate family is the largest, containing sixty species. Its members are intelligent animals which walk on all fours when on the ground, and have facial expressions, nostrils set close together, dagger-like canines in the males and non-prehensile tails. They are diurnal and are either largely terrestrial (baboons) or largely arboreal (monkeys). There are three species in Zimbabwe.

CHACMA BABOON, *Papio ursinus*

Shona: bveni/gudo
Ndebele: indwangu
Fig. 10 *Plate* 14

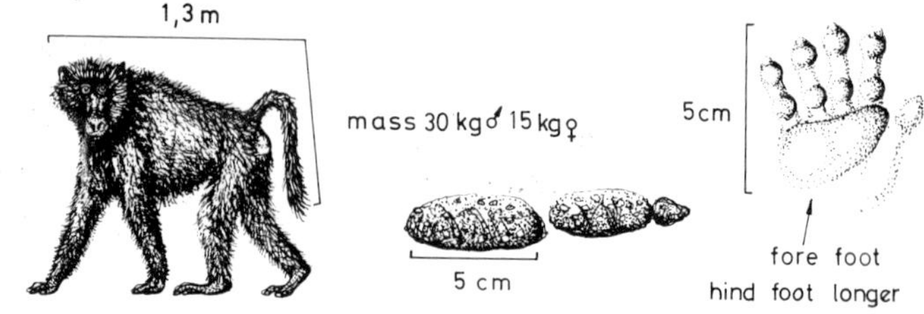

Fig. 10

Features The chacma baboon is a fairly large primate, yellowish brown in colour, with a dog-like muzzle, longish tail and coarse hair which is long on the neck and shoulders. The face is naked and the buttocks have naked callosities. Characteristically, when walking the shoulders are higher than the hips. Females are smaller than males.

Habits Chacma baboons are widely distributed in Zimbabwe, although absent or rare in some parts and more common in others (for example, the Zambezi Valley). They favour wooded country, particularly if it is broken or hilly, and are not often encountered in open expanses.

They occur in troops numbering up to a hundred individuals; occasionally more, but usually less. These troops normally have well chosen sleeping sites, in either tall trees or cliff faces, from which they descend in the early morning to start the day's wanderings in search of food. Like vervet monkeys, the distance they travel during the day in search of food depends on its availability, but in general they do not travel more than a kilometre or two away from their sleeping site. They do not always return to the same sleeping site but may have several within their home range.

Being mainly ground-dwellers, baboons are vulnerable to predation. They are therefore particularly alert and have very good eyesight and hearing. When danger threatens, the vulnerable members cluster in the centre of the group, around the most dominant and protective males, while other males surround the group, moving ahead, behind and along its sides. These are the males which normally give the alarm bark if something is spotted. Baboons will also associate with other animals, like antelope, whose alertness supplements their own. In addition to the alarm bark, baboons can grunt, growl, shriek, chatter and roar.

They are omnivorous, although largely vegetarian, feeding on wild fruits, berries, leaves, grasses, roots, bulbs and tubers as well as a variety of animal foods such as insects, scorpions, centipedes, lizards, small birds, and even small or young mammals. They are also destructive crop raiders.

Breeding The mother gives birth to a single young after a gestation period of between six and seven months, and thereafter does not breed again for about eighteen months. Breeding takes place throughout the year. The young often ride 'jockey' fashion on the mother's back, or cling on underneath.

Distribution Chacma baboons are confined to the southern part of the continent, extending from the Cape north only as far as Zambia and Angola. Beyond these northern limits, their place is taken by the yellow baboon. There are eight species of baboon in Africa.

SAMANGO MONKEY, *Cercopithecus albogularis*

Shona: dongonda
Ndebele: insimango
Other names: blue monkey, Moloney's monkey, mitis monkey
Fig. 11 *Plate* 11

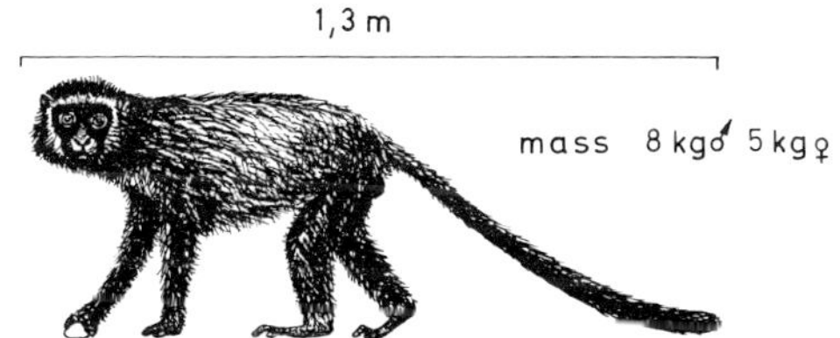

Fig. 11

Features The samango monkey is larger and darker in colour than the vervet, and in Zimbabwe is found only in the forests of the Eastern Highlands. The general colour is blue-grey, with the limbs, lower end of the tail and face darker than the rest of the body.

Habits Samango monkeys, in contrast to their cousins the vervets, spend most of their time in trees and not so much time foraging on the ground. As a result they have a better reputation than the vervets as they are not as inclined to raid vegetable gardens and croplands. They are, in fact, very much restricted to their forest type habitat and have been unable to move into and colonise new habitats, as has the vervet. Possibly they are too dependent on shade as a habitat requirement.

Samango monkeys are largely vegetarian, feeding on fruits, berries, flowers, leaves and other vegetable matter, but also eating insects and raiding birds' nests for the eggs or the fledglings. Bushbuck and blue duiker are attracted to a feeding troop of samango monkeys in the hope of picking up fallen and discarded fruits, leaves and flowers. Bushbuck, in fact, are known to eat the droppings of samango monkeys, as these are rich in undigested seeds. Both crowned eagles and leopards prey on these monkeys.

Breeding A single young is born towards the end of the year, from about September to December.

Distribution Samango monkeys are confined mainly to the southern and eastern parts of Africa, from Natal northwards to Somalia and west to Uganda.

VERVET MONKEY, *Cercopithecus pygerythrus*

Shona: tsoko/shoko
Ndebele: inkawu
Other names: black-faced monkey, grivet monkey (East Africa), green monkey (West Africa)
Fig. 12 *Plate* 13

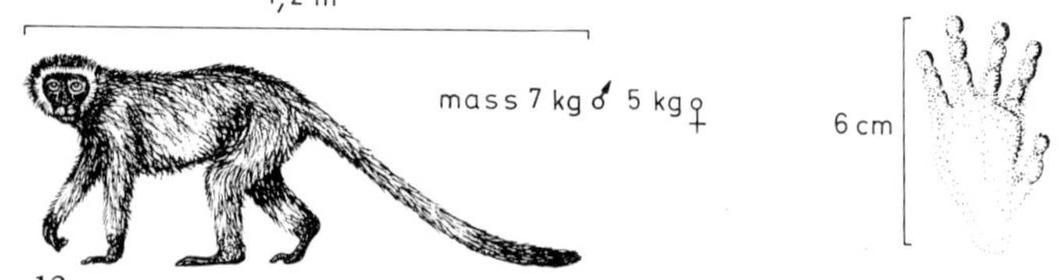

Fig. 12

Features Vervets are the well known, common grey monkeys with black faces, which are found throughout the country. They may be seen either in trees or foraging on the ground. A distinguishing feature is the band of white hair across the forehead and on the sides of the face. The hands and feet and lower half of the tail are darker than the rest of the body.

Habits Vervets are very successful primates, being able to live in a wide variety of habitats, from montane or riverine forest to the drier bush savannas. They owe their success to the fact that they are not strictly arboreal but readily take to the ground in order to search for food or to drink. As a result of this habit they frequently become garden raiders and are therefore persecuted.

They are generally found in troops numbering up to twenty individuals, although much larger groups can be found. These troops have a well defined home range over which they wander in search of food. The scarcer the food the greater this range becomes.

Their diet is very catholic although, like samangos, they are basically vegetarian, eating wild fruits, berries, leaves, young shoots, roots and bulbs, as well as insects, birds, eggs, scorpions and in fact virtually anything edible.

During the days of 'Operation Noah', rescuers were amazed to discover that not only could these monkeys swim very well, they could also dive, frequently eluding their pursuers by plunging to depths of four metres or more. Apart from man, their enemies include leopards, pythons and eagles.

Breeding Young are apparently born throughout the year but with a greater number of births taking place in the second half of the year. Females give birth to a single young (occasionally two) in their third year, and thereafter have a baby annually.

Distribution Vervets are widely distributed in Africa from the southern Cape to northern Egypt. They are easily the most widely found of all the monkeys.

Order Pholidota: pangolins

Pangolins were at one time placed in the order Edentata along with the aardvark, armadillos, sloths and anteaters. They have now been placed in a separate order as zoologists have realised they were not related to the other anteaters. The name *pholidota* means 'scaly ones'.

There are seven species of pangolins, three occurring in Asia and the remaining four occurring in Africa. The African pangolins are the giant pangolin, the tree pangolin, the long-tailed pangolin and the Cape pangolin. The tree pangolin and the long-tailed pangolin are arboreal while the giant pangolin and the Cape pangolin are terrestrial.

There is only one species in Zimbabwe, the Cape pangolin, which belongs to the single family Manidae.

CAPE PANGOLIN, *Manis temmincki*
Shona: haka/hambakubvu
Ndebele: inkakha
Other names: scaly anteater, Temminck's pangolin, ground pangolin
Fig. 13 *Plate* 6

Fig. 13

Features The pangolin is easily recognised since, unlike any other mammal, it is almost entirely covered by large overlapping scales and rather resembles a reptile. The head is small and pointed, the tail broad and flat, and the front feet are well clawed. The hind foot has only small claws and a rounded pad, rather like an elephant.

Habits Pangolins are essentially animals of dry bush country with sandy soils and, although they are widespread in Zimbabwe, they do not usually occur in the higher, wetter regions. One has been recorded in the Inyanga National Park, however. They are mainly noctural, but may often be seen during the day. They hide in holes or in other secluded places.

Pangolins eat termites and ants which are dug from their nests or scratched out from amongst detritus or dead wood. They are known to pick up pieces of termite-ridden wood and break these open onto their stomachs as they lie on their backs, licking up the insects with their darting tongues. They also scratch in animal droppings for termites. Their sense of smell is very important in locating food, and digging may be preceded by much sniffing in a particular spot. Certain species of ants or termites are not eaten, while others are favoured. Unlike the antbear, they do not have teeth but instead possess a strong muscular stomach which grinds up the food with the help of gravel they swallow when feeding.

They walk on their back legs only, with the tail raised and the front feet occasionally touching the ground. They also have a habit of standing up on the back legs to look around, and if danger threatens they may freeze into immobility or roll themselves into a tight ball, completely protecting their soft underparts. If interfered with in this position they may attempt to injure their attacker by scything the tail across the body.

Breeding Only one young is born after a gestation period of almost five months. The scales of the newborn harden in about two days. The young are often carried on the mother's lower back, or clasped to her chest and enfolded by her body if danger threatens.

Distribution This species occurs widely in southern Africa and also north to Uganda, Kenya and the Sudan.

Order Carnivora: carnivores

The carnivores are world-wide in distribution (except for the Antarctic and some ocean islands) and occur in a variety of shapes and sizes, from a weasel weighing only a few grams to the enormous brown bear of Alaska, weighing several hundred kilograms. Nevertheless, since they are primarily adapted for the killing and eating of prey, one finds they all have certain characteristics in common.

The teeth, for example, follow a basic pattern of strong incisors (for tearing and biting), well developed canines (for killing) and cheek teeth adapted either for cutting or grinding and chewing, depending on the diet of the animal. Pure flesh eaters, for example the cats, have cutting cheek teeth (called carnassials) and only vestigial grinding teeth, whereas in the more omnivorous bears and dogs the carnassials are not as well developed as are the grinding cheek teeth. The carnassial teeth do not meet but shear past each other like scissors.

Claws are important for carnivores, either for attack or defence, for holding down prey or food, or for good purchase on the ground or in trees, hence all carnivores have claws, even the clawless otter, although in the latter the claws are vestigial. The cats, highly specialised killers, have claws which are very sharp. They are enclosed in a sheath for their protection, but can be extended at will. The cheetah, which runs down its prey, has dog-like claws for a good grip on the ground. These cannot be retracted. Claws require digits to hold them and hence one never finds less than four toes on each foot.

Carnivores have well developed senses, mainly of hearing and scent, but in some, like the cheetah, eyesight is particularly good. Scent glands are well developed in some carnivores and are used for a variety of purposes, including defence, as in skunks and polecats, for marking out territories or for recognition purposes.

Some are nocturnal, others diurnal. Some are solitary while others associate in groups. The social types have developed complex patterns of behaviour and communication between members (submissive expressions and postures, for example) which ensure that conflict is kept to a minimum. Play in the young is often related to the later way of life. Kittens, for example, stalk and pounce on each other, whereas the young aardwolf's play is mainly related to escape, since aardwolves grow into timid and inoffensive animals.

Carnivores are divided into two distinct groups, depending on the structure of bones surrounding the middle and inner parts of the ear. In the one group are the cat-like carnivores, the cats, hyaenas, civets, mongooses and genets; the other group contains the dog-like carnivores such as the dogs, bears, otters, weasels and badgers.

There are about two hundred and fifty species of carnivores altogether, of which Zimbabwe has thirty species divided into six families.

Family Canidae: jackals, foxes, dogs

Canids are deep-chested, long-limbed carnivores with bushy tails, long muzzles, erect ears, and a large number of well developed teeth. They have five toes on the fore foot and four on the hind, except for the wild dog, which has four and four. They are, essentially, running mammals, with good hearing and an exceptional sense of smell.

BAT-EARED FOX, *Otocyon megalotis*

Shona: ?/gava
Ndebele: unga (?)
Other names: delalandis fox, long-eared or big-eared fox
Fig. 14 *Plate* 16

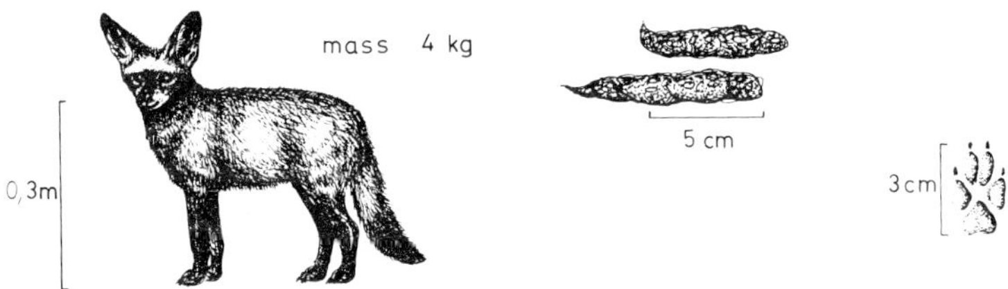

Fig. 14

Features The bat-eared fox looks rather like a small jackal. Distinguishing features are the large black-edged ears, the blackish legs, feet and muzzle, and the black-tipped tail. The overall colour is silvery buff.

Habits Bat-eared foxes are primarily nocturnal animals although, when undisturbed, they are also diurnal. They occur in pairs or larger parties, and inhabit the drier western parts of the country. They may be extending their range to the south and south-east of Zimbabwe. They live in disused antbear holes, or in burrows which they dig themselves and which may be up to three metres long.

They are mainly insect eaters, but their diet is varied and includes scorpions, sun-spiders, wild fruits, seeds, reptiles and rodents. This rather omnivorous diet has led to a reduction of the cutting cheek teeth and the development of crushing molars. The large and sensitive ears are used to locate the sounds of underground insects and larvae. These are then rapidly dug up, even through the hardest soil, with the forepaws. The ears also serve the purpose of assisting in heat loss.

They are extraordinarily nimble creatures, capable of doubling back on their tracks at a high speed, and twisting and dodging as they run. This skill, which earned them the Afrikaans name 'draai jakkal' or turning jackal, enables them to run down and catch small elusive animals, and also assists their escape from predators. The call is a rather shrill and repetitive 'who-who-who'.

Breeding Up to five young are born during the rainy season in the safety of the burrows after a gestation period of approximately two months.

Distribution They occur in the drier areas of Angola, Botswana and South West Africa, and thence from Tanzania northwards to the Sudan and Ethiopia.

SIDE-STRIPED JACKAL, *Canis adustus*

Shona: gava/gava
Ndebele: ikhanka (?)
Fig. 15 (1) *Plate* 18

Features This is rather a drab jackal, greyish in colour, with a faint black and white stripe along the side, from which it gets its name. The tip of the tail is white, whereas in the black-backed jackal it is black. This white is sometimes particularly conspicuous and bright before the onset of winter.

Habits These jackals are widespread in Zimbabwe, although not often seen because of their nocturnal habits. They are sometimes noticed before sundown, but shortly after or before sunrise they are usually hidden in thickets or antbear holes, and they are usually seen singly or in pairs. At Hwange, one may see them during the day.

Their diet is very catholic and includes rats and mice, insects such as beetles and termites, reptiles, carrion, birds and even wild fruits, such as the 'muhacha' and 'mahobohobo' fruits. In agricultural areas they are known to eat mealies, groundnuts, sunflower seeds, and so on. Their diet depends largely on what is most commonly available. Unlike the black-backed jackal, they are not known to be stock thieves and, considering their rodent eating habits, they are probably a useful species.

They usually occur singly or in pairs and are generally fairly silent animals, occasionally uttering a series of barks or yelps.

Breeding The young, numbering six or more, are born before or just after the rains start, after a gestation period of about two months.

Distribution Being a savana loving species, they occur only in the northern parts of South Africa and then north from Zimbabwe through Zambia to East Africa, the Sudan and across to West Africa.

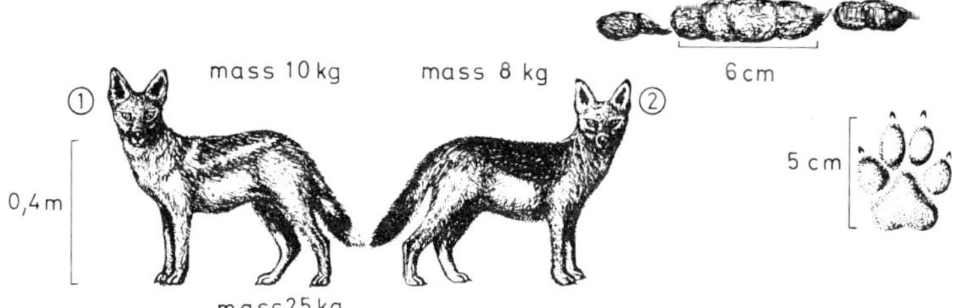

Fig. 15 (1) Side-striped jackal (2) Black-backed jackal

BLACK-BACKED JACKAL, *Canis mesomelas*

Shona: hungubwe/gava
Ndebele: ikhanka
Other name: saddle-backed jackal
Fig. 15 (2) *Plate* 15

Features This is a more attractive jackal than the side-striped jackal. It may be recognised by the reddish body colour, the black 'saddle' on the back and the black-tipped tail. The tail of the side-striped jackal is white-tipped.

Habits These jackals are not as nocturnal as are the side-striped jackals and, in areas where they are not persecuted, for example the Hwange National Park, they can often be seen trotting about in daytime. They are fairly widespread, although they do not occur in the Zambezi Valley. They appear to have a preference for open country although their habitat tolerance is fairly wide. The black-backed is a noisier species than the side-striped jackal and its howling bark, combined with that of others, often forms a nocturnal symphony pleasing to the ears of bush-lovers. These jackals occur singly, in pairs, or occasionally in larger parties.

The diet is similar to that of the side-striped jackal and includes rats and mice, other small mammals, reptiles (mainly lizards), insects (dung-beetles for example), carrion, sun-spiders, scorpions, and wild fruits. In South Africa, particularly in the Transvaal, they have become predators of sheep and stringent efforts are made to control them. Their predatory habits on livestock and poultry are unfortunate as they probably do a lot of good in the control of rodents. In game areas they frequently follow lion prides, gathering in numbers and snatching morsels from the lion kills. They also kill their own larger prey, usually the young of antelope. In captivity, the female is known to regurgitate meat to her young. They do not appear to be particularly dependent on water as they have been recorded in very arid parts of Botswana.

Breeding From four to nine young are born in a safe and secluded spot during summer.

Distribution They are common in South Africa, absent from Zambia, and present again in East Africa north to Ethiopia and the Sudan.

WILD DOG, *Lycaon pictus*
Shona: mhumhi/bumhi
Ndebele: iganyana, idlelaphezulu
Fig. 16 *Plate* 19

Fig. 16

Features This animal is easily recognised by its typical dog-like appearance, black, yellow and white speckled body, large rounded ears and white-tipped bushy tail.

Habits Wild dogs live in packs numbering from three or four individuals up to, occasionally, fifty or more. They are entirely carnivorous animals, running down their prey and devouring the victim in a matter of moments. They occur in areas where game is plentiful. They normally prey on the smaller to medium-sized antelope (although they are capable of preying on the larger antelope). In the Kruger for example, their main prey is impala, while in the Kafue National Park, although fifty prey species were recorded, reedbuck and duiker were most frequently killed. In Hwange, Ted Davison notes that reedbuck and young tsessebe were frequently killed. However, he also notes a case where they had treed a leopard, and Reay Smithers recalls an incident in Botswana where wild dogs attacked one of their own pack that had been hit by a vehicle.

Normally, however, their social behaviour is well ordered, with definite hierarchies existing to ensure that each animal knows his place, thus reducing conflict. A hunt is usually preceded by activities such as muzzle licking and bouts of playing which cause general excitement in the group. Different individuals may take up the lead in a hunt, the rest falling behind and cutting off any doubling back of the prey. They approach their intended victim with a slow walk, moving into top speed only when the victim takes flight. The prey is eventually felled by bites and then torn to pieces by the hungry dogs. A record exists of two reedbuck ewes being reduced to a pile of bones by a pack of about forty dogs in slightly less than ten minutes. They have a deep hoarse bark, while the young whine and yelp like puppies.

Breeding Breeding takes place in the dry season and the young are usually reared in antbear holes. Normally two to eight pups are born; more have occasionally been recorded. The parents regurgitate meat for the pups once they have been weaned.

Distribution Wild dogs occur from South West Africa and the Transvaal, north to Somalia, Ethiopia and the Sudan, and then westwards south of the Sahara.

Family Mustelidae: polecat, weasel, honey badger, otter

This family has many representatives distributed all over the world, including such well known animals as weasels, skunks, pine-martins, stoats, ferrets, minks, polecats, badgers and otters. They are small to medium-sized carnivores, generally long-bodied, short-legged, agile and alert. Some, like the skunks, are well known for their scent producing glands, while others produce valuable furs. They are better known in Europe and America, but, nevertheless, there are quite a few species in Africa, four of which occur in Zimbabwe. These are the clawless otter, honey badger, the polecat and the African weasel.

STRIPED POLECAT, *Ictonyx striatus*

Shona: chidembo/chidembo
Ndebele: ıqaqa
Other names: zorilla, African skunk, Cape polecat, stinkmuishond
Fig. 17 (1) *Plate* 17

Features This is a black animal with distinctive white stripes on the sides and a largely white tail. The head is black with a prominent white patch on the forehead and two further white patches between the eyes and ears on the sides of the face. It is larger than the African weasel, lacking the latter's sinuous body shape and having very much longer fur.

Habits This species has a wide habitat tolerance and is known to occur in arid areas such as the Kalahari as well as wetter areas such as the Eastern Districts of Zimbabwe. However, although widespread, they are not particularly common animals and, as they are mostly nocturnal in their habits, they are seldom seen. They generally occur alone or in pairs.

During the day they hide up in holes, hollow trees, thick bush, and even suitable hide-aways under houses.

They eat invertebrates and vertebrates, including rats, mice, reptiles, birds, frogs, insects, scorpions, sun-spiders, centipedes and eggs. They also attack poultry. The food is masticated very thoroughly before it is eaten.

The polecat, like the American skunk, is a good example of an animal having conspicuous colours in order to 'warn' a potential attacker that the animal is inedible, because of the nauseous ejection from its anal glands. When threatened, the polecat turns its back to the attacker, raises its hair, and squirts a powerful jet at the attacker, at the same time giving voice to an unpleasant high pitched scream. It will also sham death.

Breeding Two to three young are born. These are marked like the adults, but have shorter fur. They make good pets if raised from a young age.

Distribution They are widely distributed in Africa from the Cape to the Sahara, but are absent in the wetter forest regions of central West Africa.

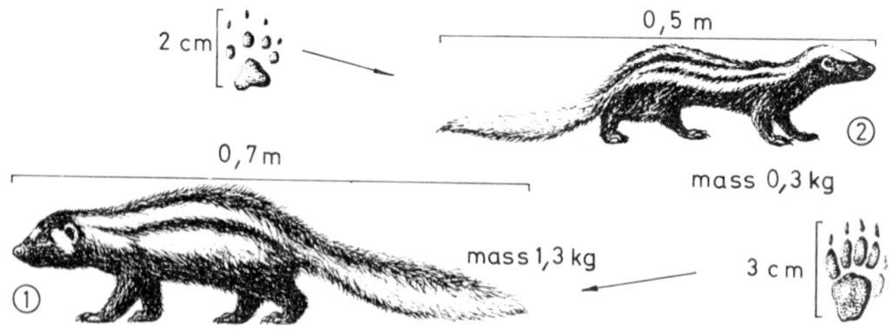

Fig. 17 (1) Striped polecat (2) African striped weasel

AFRICAN STRIPED WEASEL, *Poecilogale albinucha*
Shona: ?
Ndebele: ?
Other names: white-naped weasel, snake polecat, South African weasel, slangmuishond
Fig. 17 (2)

Plate 24 Clawless otter *National Tourist Board*

Plate 25 Meller's mongoose *Dale Kenmuir*

Plate 26 Selous' mongoose *Dale Kenmuir*

Plate 27 Slender mongoose *Dale Kenmuir*

Plate 28 Dwarf mongoose *Dale Kenmuir*

Plate 29 Banded mongoose *Alan Kemp*

Plate 30 Large grey mongoose *H. Van Rompaey*

Plate 31 Water mongoose *Dale Kenmuir*

Plate 32 White-tailed mongoose *Dale Kenmuir*

Plate 33 Rusty-spotted genet *Dale Kenmuir*

Plate 34 Civet *H. Van Rompaey*

Features This is a slender and sinuous little animal with distinct white stripes on the jet black fur on the dorsal surface, and a fairly bushy white tail. The top of the head to the nape is white, hence the alternative name, white-naped weasel. It is smaller than the striped polecat with shorter silky fur and very much shorter legs.

Habits This is a little known species and most knowledge of it comes from captive specimens. Records indicate that these weasels prefer woodland or open woodland habitat, and are mainly associated with areas which have more than 500 mm of rain per annum (Mashonaland and the Eastern Districts). They are essentially nocturnal, occurring singly as well as in parties (probably family groups) of three or four animals. They are poor climbers but are particularly good diggers and excavate their own burrows. When walking, the body is held low on the ground; they run with a bobbing motion.

In captivity they readily kill and eat rats and mice and day-old chicks, but reject insects. In Natal, captive specimens rejected eggs, snakes, lizards, toads, millipedes, fruit and grain. They have good cutting cheek teeth and the indications are that in the wild they are probably wholly carnivorous, preying mainly on rats and mice. They also enter small holes readily, another indication that rodents are probably their main prey. Captive specimens were also observed to follow prey by scent. They kill their prey by biting it at the back of the head, while, at the same time, rolling the body round it. The prey is carried back to their den.

For protection they probably rely mainly on their warning colouration and the ejection of an evil smelling fluid from the anal glands. They growl and emit a sharp 'bark-scream' when angry.

Breeding Up to three young are born towards the end of the year, from October through to December. When they are older the young will follow the mother in a 'procession'.

Distribution They are known to occur from the Cape northwards to Zambia, west Tanzania, southern Zaire and Angola.

HONEY BADGER, *Mellivora capensis*

Shona: sere/tsere
Ndebele: ulinda, umantwane
Other name: ratel
Fig. 18 *Plate* 20

Features The honey badger may be recognised by its stocky badger-like shape of which the upper half is white and the lower half black.

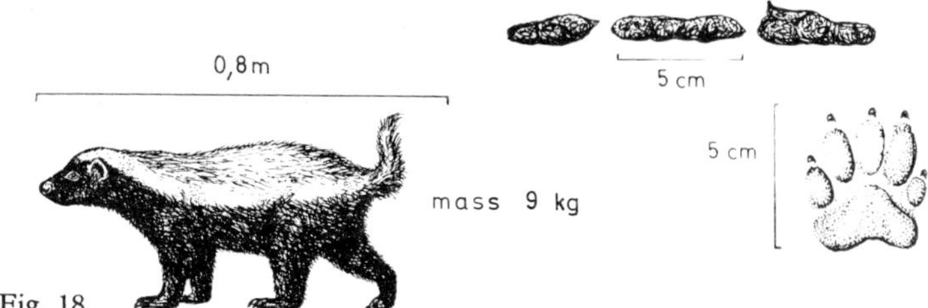

Fig. 18

The legs are short, powerful and well clawed, the tail is short and bushy, and the thick hide is covered with coarse hair.

Habits The honey badger has a wide habitat tolerance and hence occurs widely throughout Zimbabwe. They are mainly nocturnal and are usually seen alone or in pairs. They shelter during the day in old ant-bear holes, cracks, crevices and other suitable cover. Despite their superficial resemblance to true badgers, authorities regard them as being more closely related to the weasel group of this family.

They range widely when foraging and have a very omnivorous diet. Their powerful claws enable them to dig, turn over stones, tear bark away from dead trees, and even tear their way into poultry runs. Baboon-spiders, scorpions, various reptiles, insects, grubs, eggs, birds, fish, wild fruit and honey all figure largely in their diet. They may even attack antelope and a record exists of one intrepid 'badger' killing and eating a three metre python. There is good evidence that the honey badger does in fact follow the honey guide, *Indicator indicator* (see Fig. 18a), to a bee's nest, as has long been reported.

Fig. 18a Honeyguide

Honey badgers have a reputation for fearlessness and occasional ferocity. With their tough and loose hide, dangerous teeth and long strong claws, they are formidable opponents when aroused, and can hold their own against several dogs. In Botswana, Reay Smithers recalls an incident where a honey badger destroyed a steel live-trap it had been caught in, returning to further mangle the trap after it had ripped its way out. They may secrete a strong smelling liquid from the anal glands which further deters the enemy. Their bold and conspicuous black and white colour pattern serves to warn off potential attackers that the animal in question is a ratel and therefore best left alone. (Skunks and polecats also carry a warning colouration.) They growl, grunt and utter a high pitched scream-bark when suddenly disturbed.

Breeding Usually two young are born, probably in summer. They make good pets; one specimen has been recorded as living in captivity for twenty-four years.

Distribution They occur widely throughout Africa up to the Sahara, and also in parts of the Middle East and in India.

CLAWLESS OTTER, *Aonyx capensis*

Shona: binza, mbiti
Ndebele: intini
Other names: small-clawed otter, Cape clawless otter
Fig. 19 *Plate* 24

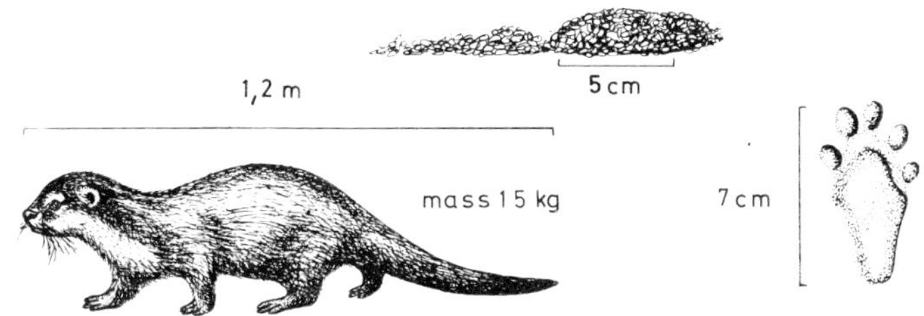

Fig. 19

Features This is the only otter known to occur in Zimbabwe, although the spotted-necked otter (*Lutra maculicollis*) may occur in the Zambezi in the north-west of Zimbabwe. They are solidly built animals with thick pointed tails, blunt heads, small rounded ears, long whiskers, and a distinct moustache. The overall colour is dark brown with white chest, throat and sides of face. The name derives from the fact that the fore feet have no claws while the hind feet have only small vestigial claws and are only partially webbed (see Fig. 19a).

Fig. 19a Hind foot of clawless otter

Habits The clawless otter is both diurnal and nocturnal and is found alone, in pairs, or in small family parties. They occur widely in Rhodesia, from the streams, rivers and dams of the lowveld up to the streams and dams of the Eastern Highlands.

In captivity, otters are well known for the dexterity of their fingers; this is related to their feeding habits in the wild where they search under rocks and in the nooks and crannies of the river bed for crabs, molluscs and other edible foods. The well developed crushing molars are adapted for dealing with hard shelled foods such as crabs and mussels, but the diet also includes fish, frogs, terrapins, leguaans, insects, aquatic birds, rodents, and even poultry. With fish, the scales, fins and intestines are all eaten. Well developed canines enable them to deal effectively with small mammals and birds. Their hearing and sense of smell is acute. They do not confine themselves to water but often travel fair distances inland in search of food. They are very good swimmers.

In captivity they utter a variety of noises including squeaks, growls, whines, hisses, screams and whistles.

Breeding Their lairs and resting places are found in thick vegetation alongside the water, in riverside holes, or in crevices amongst boulders. The entrance to the lair may be underwater. Two to four pups are born in these retreats during March or April, after a gestation period of about two months.

Distribution They occur widely in Africa, from the Cape to Ethiopia and across to West Africa.

Family Viverridae: civets, genets, mongooses

These are small to medium-sized carnivores characterised by having long low bodies, short legs, long and usually well furred tails, and long faces with a large number of teeth. Nearly all have scent glands which secrete a strong-smelling fluid. They differ from the cat family in having a fifth toe on the hind foot, in having non-retractile claws and having more teeth (thirty-six to forty) than do the cats (thirty). They are mostly nocturnal and many are agile and graceful in their movements.

There are seventy-five species in all, and these are found in southern Europe, Africa, Malagasy and Asia. The mongooses are essentially African in distribution. Zimbabwe has fourteen species of viverrids, if one includes the yellow mongoose, *Cynictis penicillata*, which probably occurs in Hwange.

TREE CIVET, *Nandinia binotata*

Shona: ?
Ndebele: ?
Other names: palm civet, two-spotted palm civet
Fig. 20

0,7 m

mass 2 kg

Fig. 20

Features This is an arboreal species which looks rather like a robust furry genet. The brown woolly fur has faint dorsal spots, the thick tail is ringed, and there is a pair of light spots above the shoulder blades (hence the alternative name).

Habits Tree civets are uncommon and occur only in the evergreen forests in the Eastern Districts, where they lead an arboreal and nocturnal existence. They are adapted to a life in the trees and have short legs and sharp curved claws. Whereas the other tree civets occurring in Africa have a dentition adapted mainly for a vegetarian diet, the species occurring here has reasonably well developed cutting cheek teeth, indicating that they prey on smaller animals.

In fact, the little that is known about their feeding habits indicates that they eat fruit as well as small animals such as birds, rodents, and bats; there is a record elsewhere of one attacking a half-grown sleeping monkey. Thus it would appear that they are fairly active predators.

An interesting adaptation of this species to tree life is the position of the scent glands which are ventral and pregenital. This enables them to 'leave their mark' on a branch by simply lowering the body onto the branch and dragging it forward slightly.

Breeding Very little is known of the breeding habits of this species. Records exist of young being born in September.

Distribution This species occurs as far north as Kenya, and then west through Zaire and central West Africa to West Africa.

CIVET, *Civettictis civetta*

Shona: bvungo/jachacha
Ndebele: insimba
Other names: civet cat, African civet
Fig. 21 *Plate* 34

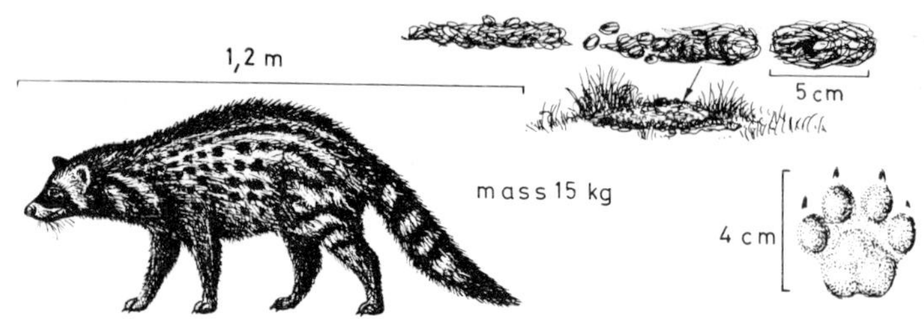

Fig. 21

Features The civet is the largest member of the viverrid group. It is an attractive animal with an overall grey shaggy coat overlain by black spots on the body and black stripes on the tail and neck region. The tail is fairly bushy and pointed, black on top, black and white ringed below. The face is characterised by a black mask across the eyes. The limbs are black and fairly short and the rather pointed head is carried low, the back sloping towards the head.

Habits Civets are widespread in Zimbabwe, being common in rocky savanna country particularly where water is available in some form or other. Like most of the viverrids, they are nocturnal, occur solitarily or in pairs, and lie up during the day in thick cover or old antbear holes. They have the habit of depositing their droppings in middens.

Their diet is very catholic and includes rats, mice, birds, snakes, frogs, hares, the young of small buck, insects, sun-spiders, chongololos, birds' eggs and wild fruit (such as marulas and batoka plums). Their middens are, in fact, most interesting; they are likely to be composed of a big mass of chongololo shells, fruit pips, bones, feathers, insect remains and other odds and ends. The droppings are particularly large in diameter. Civets wander widely when feeding.

The secretion of their scent glands, which looks like rancid butter, is known as 'civet' and has long been used in the manufacture of the best perfumes. These glands may play some part in helping the male to locate a female, as in captive animals mating is preceded by a great deal of scent marking. When threatened they erect their dorsal mane and secrete from the glands. They also growl deeply and give a fairly sharp cough.

Breeding Breeding takes place towards the end of the year when up to four young are born in a secluded place. They are weaned at about five months.

Distribution They occur widely in Africa, northwards from the Transvaal to south of the Sahara, and across to Senegal in West Africa.

SMALL-SPOTTED GENET, *Genetta genetta*

Shona: tsimba/simba
Ndebele: insimba
Other names: European or common genet
Fig. 22 (1) *Plate* 35

Features This animal is very similar to the rusty-spotted genet but is distinguished by a crest of black hair along the back, a longer coarser coat, more black on the hind feet, darker body spots, and usually a white-tipped tail (as opposed to the black-tipped tail of the rusty-spotted genet).

Habits Like the rusty-spotted genets they are mainly solitary animals, nocturnal, terrestrial, and partly arboreal. They have a wide habitat tolerance, occurring in riverine forest as well as dry scrub savanna and they are independent of surface water, as they occur even in arid parts of Botswana.

During the day they hide in holes or other retreats and venture out only after dark. They are occasionally seen in pairs. They readily take to trees when disturbed, climbing to the topmost branches and remaining there even when powerful lights are shone on them.

The diet of these active little predators is similar to that of their cousin, and includes rats and mice, snakes, lizards, geckos, insects, scorpions, sun-spiders, birds, frogs and wild fruits. Rats and mice are probably their main food. They also raid poultry runs.

Breeding The young are born during the wet summer months, or just preceding them. From two to four young are born.

Distribution This species is widely distributed in Africa, occurring from the southern edge of the Sahara, south to the Cape. They also occur in parts of the Middle East, Spain and France and other parts of Europe.

RUSTY-SPOTTED GENET, *Genetta tigrina*

Shona: tsimba/simba
Ndebele: insimba
Other name: large-spotted genet
Fig. 22 (2) *Plate* 33

Features Both species of genet are very similar in general appearance and size. The rusty-spotted genet, however, has a black-tipped tail, as opposed to the white-tipped tail of its cousin, and it also lacks the spinal crest which the small-spotted genet has. Other differences are the

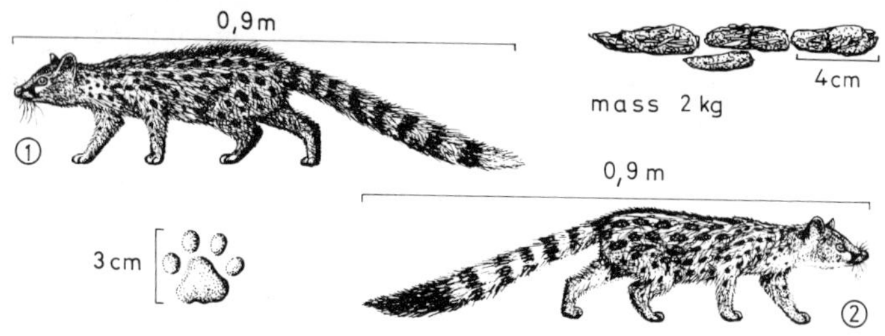

Fig. 22 (1) Small-spotted genet (2) Rusty-spotted genet

shorter fur and the reduced amount of black on the back feet. As the name implies, the spots are a rusty colour.

Habits These are solitary, nocturnal animals which hide by day in secluded places and emerge after dark to hunt. One frequently sees them on the road at night, slipping away into the grass. They are widespread occurring in woodlands, scrub-bush or around rocky kopjes; however, they appear to be more closely associated with water than does the small-spotted genet which is known to occur in very arid areas (for example in Botswana).

They are voracious little predators, particularly favouring rats and mice but, like most small predators, their diet is very catholic and includes birds, eggs, reptiles, frogs, insects, sun-spiders, scorpions, spiders and even wild fruits. Small vertebrates are killed by a series of bites directed at the neck. They are also skilled poultry thieves, and are able to slip through even the smallest of gaps in a chicken run. In Natal they have been reported as stealing small crocodiles from a crocodile farm.

Breeding Young are born from August to February in holes, hollow logs, or other secluded places, and litter numbers range from three to five. The eyes open about ten days after birth. The initial dark grey spots turn reddish only when the genet is several months old.

Distribution They are widely distributed over most of Africa south of the Sahara.

LARGE GREY MONGOOSE, *Herpestes ichneumon*

Shona: ?
Ndebele: ?
Other names: ichneumon, Egyptian mongoose, greater grey mongoose
Fig. 23 (1) *Plate* 30

Features As the name implies, this is a large grey mongoose, in fact, one of the largest of all African mongooses. Distinguishing features are the black tip to the tail, blackish face, black feet, the long and coarse fur and the five toes to each foot.

Habits This species is closely associated with water, occurring in riverine forest and bush or in any thick cover not far from water. As a result they are absent from the drier western parts of Zimbabwe. Where they do occur in dry areas such as the Zambezi Valley they are confined to the riparian margins. They swim well and take to water readily if necessary.

While most of the solitary mongooses are nocturnal (with the exception of the slender mongoose), this species is mainly diurnal and is occasionally seen in pairs or in slightly larger parties. Their retreats are in secluded places such as holes, rock crevices, hollow trees, thick bush and overhanging river banks.

Their diet, as could be expected of a species living close to water, includes frogs, fish and vlei rats, as well as other small rodents, reptiles, birds and insects (such as grasshoppers and beetles). They are also known to raid poultry yards.

Breeding The available data on breeding indicates that two to four young are born.

Distribution This species is widely distributed in Africa, from the Cape northwards as far as Egypt and across to West Africa.

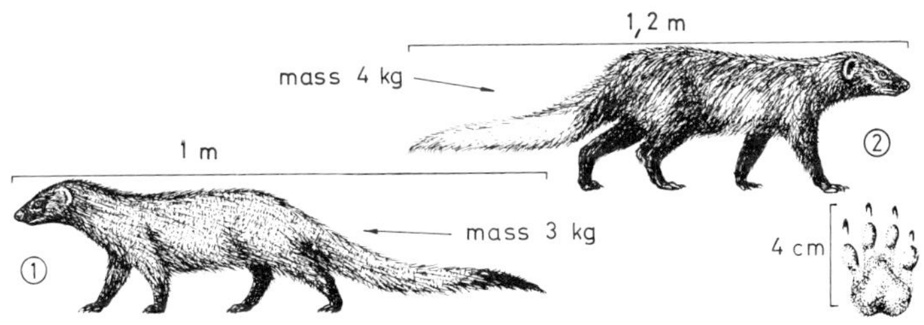

Fig. 23 (1) Large grey mongoose (2) White-tailed mongoose

WHITE-TAILED MONGOOSE, *Ichneumia albicauda*
Shona: jerenyenje
Ndebele: ubachakide
Fig. 23 (2) *Plate* 32

Features This is a large, rather shaggy-coated mongoose, distinguished by the longish legs and the white tip to the tail. The general colour is a grizzled darkish grey, with the underparts and limbs dark. Each foot has five toes; the front toes are long and curved. Selous' mongoose also has a white-tipped tail, but is much smaller and lighter in colour, and has four toes on each foot instead of five.

Habits White-tailed mongooses are nocturnal and usually solitary, or occurring in pairs. They are found in riverine bush and scrub, or generally where there is good cover in association with water where they can lie up during the day. They may also use antbear holes or any convenient hole to lie up in. They occur widely in Zimbabwe and one occasionally sees them trotting along the road at night, carrying their bodies high off the ground, the head lower than the back and hind-quarters. They are said to visit human habitations where they forage for insects attracted to lights, or for dung beetle larvae in cattle kraals.

In general they have a catholic diet that includes rodents, birds, frogs, toads, crabs, reptiles and insects, such as beetles, grasshoppers and termites. Frogs and toads in fact occur fairly constantly in their diet, indicating their preference for a riverine habitat. They are avid diggers, and earthworms and insect grubs are eaten in fair quantities. They are also inclined to raid poultry runs. When cornered, they raise their hackles, thus enlarging their appearance; they also growl, bark sharply and give a type of explosive grunt. They are not good climbers.

Breeding Two or three young are born during the summer months, from October through to February or March.

Distribution They are fairly widely distributed in Africa, occurring from the eastern Cape in South Africa, north to the Sudan and Ethiopia, and then across to West Africa. They are absent from the tropical forests of the equator and the drier parts of southern Africa.

BANDED MONGOOSE, *Mungos mungo*

Shona: dzvororo
Ndebele: usikibhororo
Other name: zebra mongoose
Fig. 24 (1) *Plate* 29

Features These mongooses are easily identified as they are diurnal and social, and will often be seen in groups. The larger size and transverse dark and light stripes on the back will distinguish them from the smaller dwarf mongoose, another diurnal, social species. The grey-brown coat is rather wiry, and the short tail tapers towards a black tip. The toes of the fore feet have long strong claws.

Habits These mongooses occur both north and south of the central watershed, below 1 200 m. They occur in groups of about five to thirty members, and are usually found in a woodland or thicket type habitat, normally where anthills provide them with a safe retreat for the night or a refuge from danger during the day.

They prefer this type of habitat because they are mainly insectivorous and can readily find food in the debris and accumulated leaf litter occurring in these areas. Also, being diurnal and relatively small, they are exposed to predation, particularly from large birds of prey, and thick bush provides them with a measure of protection. Numerous observations confirm that a group will often have several anthills or other retreats within their home range. They are liable to turn on any raptor that attempts to attack them. Their diet consists largely of insects, particularly beetle larvae and adults, but it also includes scorpions, sun-spiders, birds' eggs, reptiles, rodents, snails and wild fruit. They break birds' eggs by rolling them through their back legs against a handy rock.

They chatter when feeding and if disturbed utter a rather shrill chitter, standing up on their back legs to peer around.

Breeding Up to three young are born from October through to February, after a gestation period of about two months. One mother may look after and suckle several litters while the other mothers go out to feed.

Distribution They occur widely in the woodland savannas of southern Africa, north to the Sudan and Somalia and then across to Nigeria.

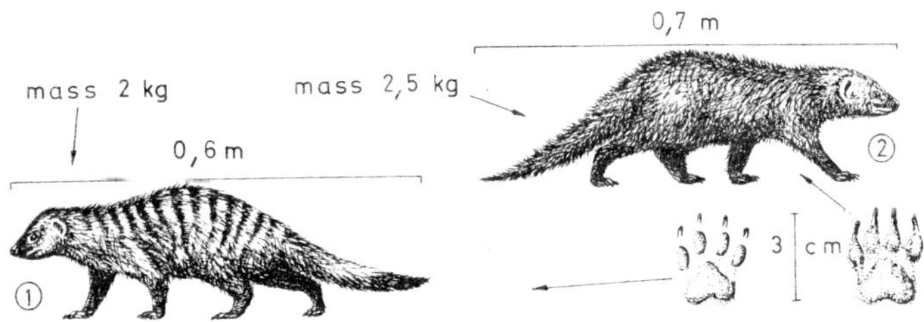

Fig. 24 (1) Banded mongoose (2) Water mongoose

WATER MONGOOSE, *Atilax paludinosus*

Shona: chidzvororo
Ndebele: imvuzi
Other name: marsh mongoose
Fig. 24 (2) *Plate* 31

Features The water mongoose is a fairly robust dark brown mongoose with a rather coarse shaggy coat and a short tapering tail. The colour may vary in intensity from one animal to the next. The feet each have five long slender toes. These mongooses are good swimmers, readily taking to water, and at a distance can be mistaken for otters.

Habits As the name implies, this species lives in thick bush and scrub in the vicinity of streams, rivers, swamps, vleis and dams. They are not particularly common in Zimbabwe and are seldom seen because of their nocturnal habits, although their presence may be betrayed by their tell-tale spoor in the mud. They occur mainly in the eastern half of the country, from the lower altitudes up to the heights of the Eastern Districts.

Their food consists of aquatic animals such as crabs, fish, frogs and tadpoles, as well as rats and mice (such as the veli rat), reptiles, birds, insects (such as beetles and termites) and wild fruit. They are also known to dig up and eat crocodiles' eggs. The long thin and mobile fingers of this species are adapted, like those of the clawless otter, to feeling around in the water and mud for small animals, such as crabs and frogs. The cheek teeth are robust and well adapted for crushing hard foods, such as crabs and beetles. They wander widely in search of food and occasionally raid inland poultry runs.

If disturbed they are likely to emit a strong musky smell from the anal glands. The scent from these glands is also used for marking territory. Under stress they also growl, blow loudly through the nose and emit an explosive bark.

Breeding Breeding takes place at the end of the year, when two or three young are born in well sheltered places.

Distribution They are widely distributed in Africa although they are more common south of the equator than north of it; they do not occur in the drier areas.

SELOUS' MONGOOSE, *Paracynictis selousi*

Shona: jerenyenje
Ndebele: u(bu)chakide
Fig. 25 (1) *Plate* 26

Features This is an attractive medium-sized mongoose, recognised by the overall white-grey colour, the dark or blackish legs, and the white tip to the tail.

Habits They are nocturnal and occur singly or in pairs. They are interesting in that, unlike other mongooses, they excavate their own burrows, which extend several metres below the surface and have numerous tunnels and entrances, the latter usually in the cover of bushes. The long curved claws of this species are an adaptation for their digging habits. Because of this burrowing habit they have a preference for sandy soils and are usually found in open woodlands and scrub.

They are widespread in Zimbabwe, although absent from the Eastern Districts.

Their diet is varied, including a variety of insects, particularly beetles and their larvae, termites, sun-spiders, scorpions, and small vertebrates such as rats and mice, lizards, snakes, frogs, birds and baby crocodiles.

Breeding Up to two young are born in the safety of their burrows during the warm summer months.

Distribution This is not a widely distributed species in Africa as it occurs only south of the equator, in Zimbabwe, Zambia, Botswana, South West Africa, Angola, the Transvaal and Zululand.

Fig. 25 (1) Selous' mongoose (2) Meller's mongoose

MELLER'S MONGOOSE, *Rhynchogale melleri*

Shona: ?
Ndebele: u(bu)chakide (?)
Fig. 25 (2) *Plate* 25

Features This is a medium-sized mongoose, rather pale brown in colour with a black tip to the fairly long tail, and fairly dark feet. There are five toes to each foot, the inner ones being very small. It is closely related to the bushy-tailed mongoose but, unlike that species, does not have a naked groove from the nose to the mouth.

Habits Although it is fairly widely distributed, this species is uncommon. It is usually found associated with bush savanna.

Not a great deal is known about the Meller's mongoose. The wide blunt cheek teeth suggest a fairly omnivorous diet, rather than a purely predaceous one. Certainly, the little that is known about their diet indicates that this may be so as they are known to eat both wild fruits and termites.

Breeding Two or three young are born about November or December.

Distribution They are not widely distributed in Africa, occurring only south of the equator from the Transvaal north through Mozambique and Zambia to East Africa.

DWARF MONGOOSE, *Helogale parvula*
Shona: ?/govo
Ndebele: iduha (?)
Other name: pygmy mongoose
Fig. 26 (1) *Plate* 28

Features These are the smallest of the African mongooses. Like the banded mongoose they are diurnal and social, but they lack any distinguishing colours or marks, being a uniform brownish colour.

Habits These gregarious diurnal little mongooses are associated with tree savannas of the drier western, northern and southern parts of Zimbabwe. Anthills are most often used by troops for their permanent refuges, but they will also colonise rocky places or any other convenient safe retreat. A characteristic of their habitat is an accumulation of dead trees, branches, logs and so on where they can take temporary refuge. Permanent retreats are characterised by the collection of scats outside. Where a colony exists they will often be seen sunning themselves outside in the early morning, all the while keeping a watchful eye out for birds of prey. The alarm call is a sharp 'chu-chwee'. When disturbed they will sit up on their hind legs to look around. Troops number from three or four up to twenty or more.

From their retreats they wander out to forage in the fallen leaves and debris, maintaining contact with little chirruping noises. Insects are their main food, including beetles and their larvae, and grasshoppers, but they eat virtually anything unearthed or caught, including scorpions, spiders, sun-spiders, centipedes, rats and mice, reptiles, wild fruit and berries. Eggs are dealt with in the typical mongoose fashion, being propelled backwards through the back legs against a rock. They are independent of water. On cold or rainy days they do not normally venture out and usually return to their retreats well before sunset.

Breeding Up to four young are born after a gestation period of about fifty days. Breeding occurs towards the end and at the beginning of the year during the summer months. The young purr as they suckle.

Distribution They occur from Natal, north to Somalia and Ethiopia, and in Botswana, Angola and South West Africa. They are more common south of the equator than north of it.

SLENDER MONGOOSE, *Herpestes sanguineus*
Shona: hovo/govo
Ndebele: iwobo
Other names: red mongoose, black-tipped mongoose, lesser mongoose
Fig. 26 (2) *Plate* 27

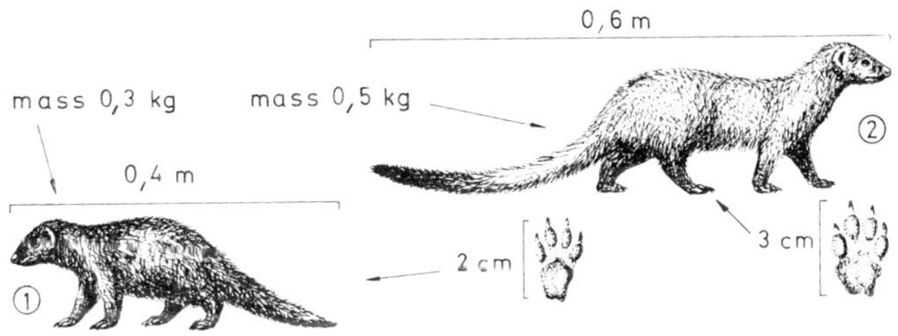

Fig. 26 (1) Dwarf mongoose (2) Slender mongoose

Features This is a slender animal, reddish in colour and with a tail ending in a distinct black tip. This reddish colour may vary in intensity, depending on the locality.

Habits This is a diurnal species, normally solitary, which occurs widely in Zimbabwe wherever there is good cover such as piles of boulders, thick bush, fallen trees, scrub and so on. They are found in and around built up areas as well, provided cover is available, and they often inhabit the tunnels of termite mounds. They have a habit of darting across the road and are frequently killed by cars as a result. They characteristically walk with the tail trailing, only the black tip turned up, the nose to the ground and the back slightly arched.

They are more common in well watered areas, but are known to occur in arid regions and are obviously not greatly dependent on water. They prey on rats and mice, birds and reptiles, insects, scorpions and, occasionally, on wild fruits. By and large they are a useful species to have in your garden although they are prone to attacking unprotected chickens when opportunity arises.

A record exists of a slender mongoose attacking, killing by biting it behind the head, and partially eating a three metre black mamba. Eggs are broken by thrusting them backwards through the back legs against a hard object. The larger raptors, such as the African hawk-eagle are probably their main enemies, as birds flying overhead are watched very cautiously. If disturbed they may freeze, or rise onto the back legs to look around.

Breeding Two to three young are born in holes, crevices and other secluded places during the summer months. When they are older, young may be seen following closely behind the mother in a procession.

Distribution They are widely distributed in Africa from the Cape Province northwards to the Sahara.

BUSHY-TAILED MONGOOSE, *Bdeogale crassicauda*
Shona: ?
Ndebele: ?
Fig. 27

Fig. 27

Features This mongoose is similar in size to Meller's mongoose, but is darker, having a dark greyish-brown overall colour. It differs in that it has a naked groove from the nose to the upper lip, and it has no first (inner) toe. It has a bushy tail.

Habits Very little is known about this rare species. It has been recorded in the extreme south-east and east of Zimbabwe. It feeds on insects, rodents and possibly aquatic animals.

Distribution Outside our borders they are known from the eastern parts of Zambia and Malawi, the lower Zambezi Valley south to Gorongosa, and also in Tanzania and Kenya.

Family Protelidae: aardwolf

While many authorities still place the aardwolf in the hyaena family, the present trend is to place this species in a separate family. While aardwolves superficially resemble hyaenas, their teeth are totally different, being very small and weak and adapted for an insect eating diet. They also differ from hyaenas in being smaller and having five toes on the fore feet instead of four, as in the hyaenas. The single known species occurs only in Africa.

AARDWOLF, *Proteles cristatus*
Shona: mwena
Ndebele: inthuhu, isangci
Other name: maanhaar jakkal
Fig. 28 *Plate* 23

Features The aardwolf is about the size of a jackal but has the characteristic shape of the hyaena, with the shoulders sloping down to the back legs. Distinguishing features are the vertical stripes on the body, the thick-haired mane on the back (from which the Afrikaans

Plate 35 Small-spotted genet *National Tourist Board*

Plate 36 Wild cat *Dale Kenmuir*

Plate 37 Serval *Dale Kenmuir*

Plate 38 Leopard *A. J. S. Weaving*

Plate 39 Cheetah *Dale Kenmuir*

Plate 40 Caracal *Peter Johnson*

Plate 41 Giraffe *Russell Williams*

Plate 42 Burchell's zebra *Dale Kenmuir*

name is derived), the bushy black-tipped tail and the black muzzle. The general colour is yellowish brown or buff.

Habits The aardwolf is a timid and inoffensive animal, mainly nocturnal, hiding by day in its burrow (usually an antbear hole or a refuge dug by itself) and venturing out at night or early morning and late evening. These animals are usually seen alone, or in pairs or larger groups, which are likely to be family parties. Although widespread in Rhodesia, they are not common and are more likely to be encountered in the west than anywhere else. They prefer an open habitat.

They have reduced dentition and it is not surprising to find that their diet consists almost entirely of harvester and other termites, and occasionally other insects; spiders, sun-spiders, carrion and vegetable foods have also been recorded. The teeth, apart from the canines, are too poorly developed to deal with freshly killed meat, and there is no evidence that they kill domestic stock. They may at times range far; one animal in the western Transvaal was found to travel thirty-six kilometres in twenty-four hours.

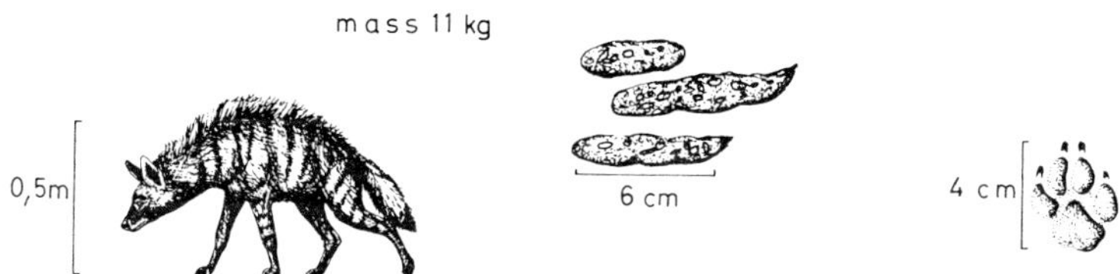

Fig. 28

For defence they erect their mane which has the effect of increasing their size suddenly, and thus has an intimidatory effect on the attacker. They are also able to utter a very loud ferocious roar, an explosive bark or a deep growl. A third method of defence is to emit a strong smelling odour from their anal glands. These glands are also used to mark territory. In captivity they cover their excreta with sand.

Breeding The young usually number up to four and are born in burrows from September to December. A lifespan of almost thirteen years has been recorded.

Distribution The species has rather a patchy distribution, occurring in southern Africa south of Zambia, and then again in East Africa from Tanzania north to the Sudan and Ethiopia.

Family Hyaenidae: hyaenas

This is a small family comprising only three species of medium-large carnivores. Although they look rather like dogs, hyaenas are in fact more closely related to the cat and civet families. Once widespread over Eurasia, they are now confined to south-west Asia and Africa.

Characteristically, they have massive heads with powerful jaw muscles, strong crushing teeth, fore legs longer than the hind legs (so that the back slopes), short tails, coarse rough fur and four toes on each foot. They have a very keen sense of smell.

Two of the three species are found in Zimbabwe.

SPOTTED HYAENA, *Crocuta crocuta*
Shona: bere/bere
Ndebele: impisi (?)
Fig. 29 (1) *Plate* 21

Features The spotted hyaena is about the size of a large dog, and has a large head, a dull yellowish coat marked by dark irregular spots, a shortish tail which ends in a black brush, a dark muzzle and dark lower limbs. Characteristically, the shoulders are heavier and stand much higher than the hindquarters. The ears are rounded, whereas those of the brown hyaena are more pointed.

Habits They have a wide habitat tolerance and are widespread in Zimbabwe, except in the more densely populated areas. They are mainly nocturnal animals with keen senses, scavenging the remains (usually bones and skin) of the prey of other predators. They normally occur singly, in pairs or in larger parties.

In recent years it has become evident that hyaenas are not only scavengers but frequently kill their own prey. In the Ngorongoro crater in East Africa, for example, hyaenas not only occur in 'social clans' numbering from ten to one hundred individuals, but they actively hunt, with the result that lions frequently scavenge on the prey of hyaenas, thus reversing the normal relationship. Where game is scarce and stock plentiful, they become a menace to livestock, and poisoning is about the only effective control measure. Under certain conditions they can become man-eaters, as occurred in the Mlanje district of Malawi in the 1950s, when Africans sleeping outside in the hot months were frequently killed by these opportunistic animals. They are also prone to scavenging around settlements, eating anything from old skins to mealie husks. They are not dependent on surface water, but will drink if it is available.

They are well known for their maniacal laughter, which occurs at times of excitement often around a kill, and also when males are attendant on a female in heat. The other well known call is a long drawn out, far-sounding 'whoo-oo-up' often heard at night. They range far;

in one case hyaenas were tracked from a goat kill to their dens forty kilometres away.

They are not hermaphrodites (bi-sexual) as is popularly supposed. The female clitoris is unusually developed, resembling the penis of a male. This, together with a pair of swellings of fibrous tissue resembling a scrotum, has given rise to this fallacy. The fact that females are larger than the males and are dominant to them has probably enhanced this belief.

Breeding The young are well developed at birth and are usually born in old antbear holes during the winter months. Up to four pups are born, dark in colour and without spots. The gestation period is about three months.

Distribution Spotted hyaenas occur throughout Africa south of the Sahara, although not in the denser forest areas of west Central Africa, and generally absent in South Africa except Zululand and the Transvaal.

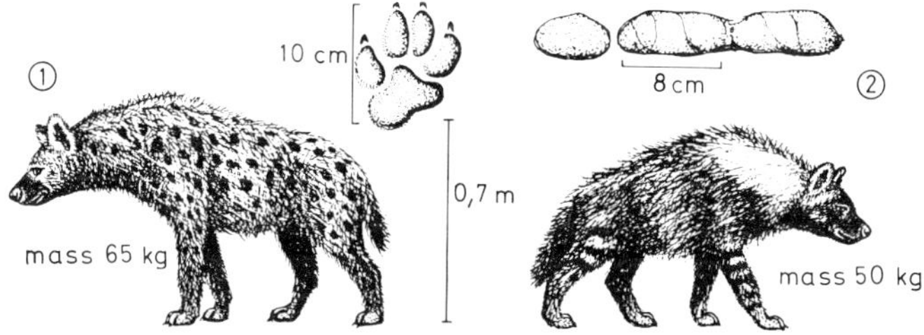

Fig. 29 (1) Spotted hyaena (2) Brown hyaena

BROWN HYAENA, *Hyaena brunnea*

Shona: bere/bere
Ndebele: impisi (?)
Other name: strandwolf
*Fig.*29 (2) *Plate* 22

Features The brown hyaena is smaller than the spotted hyaena, and has a long, shaggy brown coat, a heavy mane, a fairly bushy long tail, indistinct stripes on the legs, and no body spots. The ears are pointed whereas those of the spotted hyaena are rounded.

Habits Brown hyaenas are mainly nocturnal, occurring singly, in pairs, or small groups, and hiding up during the day in secluded places such as antbear holes or thickets, only emerging at night to wander off in search of food. They are rather rare animals and, in Zimbabwe, are found in the drier western parts where they can exist without water for months. They have a preference for dry open scrub and woodland savannas.

They scavenge carrion as well as killing their own prey, and eat a wide variety of foods, including insects, birds, eggs and wild fruits. In the Kruger National Park and in Botswana they are reported to be more predaceous than the spotted hyaenas, attacking and killing a wide range of species, including such large animals as kudu; they also attack domestic stock, a habit which has led to their decimation in many parts of South Africa. Where they occur in coastal regions they scavenge on the beaches, a habit earning them the Afrikaans name of 'strandwolf'.

Breeding The available data on breeding indicates that from one to three pups are born.

Distribution The species occurs only in Zimbabwe, South West Africa, Botswana, South Africa and Angola, although nowhere is it particularly common. It is in fact considered to be an endangered species which faces extinction.

Family Felidae: cats

The cats are highly specialised carnivores, characterised by the shortened head which has a reduced number of teeth (thirty). The canines are well developed for killing, while the cheek teeth are developed for slicing rather than chewing. With the exception of the cheetah, all cats have strong sharp retractile claws. There are five toes on the fore foot and four on the hind foot. They have an excellent sense of balance, can move extremely silently and are very strong and muscular; they have acute hearing and good eyesight.

There are thirty-four species distributed over most of the world. Zimbabwe has six species.

WILD CAT, *Felis libyca*

Shona: nhiriri/nhiriri, goya
Ndebele: igola
Other name: African wild cat
Fig. 30 *Plate* 36

Features The wild cat looks very much like the domestic tabby cat, but it is larger and has longer legs and, usually, distinguishing red fur behind the ears and at the back of the hind legs. The tail has black bands and terminates in a black tip while the legs are also distinctly marked with transverse black bands. Specimens from central and eastern Zimbabwe are darker in colour than those from the west. Males are larger than the females. The similarity to the tabby is not surprising, as

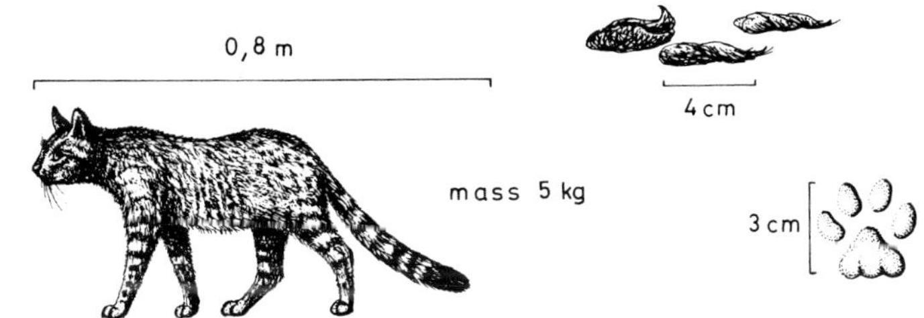

Fig. 30

authorities agree that domestic cats are descended from African wild cats which were kept in considerable numbers as pets by the ancient Egyptians.

Habits Although mainly nocturnal, hiding by day in thick cover, wild cats may also occasionally be seen during the day. They have a wide habitat tolerance, occurring even in the surrounds of built up areas and also in very dry areas. They are particularly partial to mealie fields, where their principal prey, rodents, are plentiful. In fact, man's agricultural activities, creating as they have suitable habitats for rodents, have considerably benefited the wild cat.

They feed mainly on rats and mice but also eat a wide variety of other foods, including small to large birds (doves, quail, and so on), reptiles (skinks, geckos, lizards and snakes), insects, sun-spiders, larger mammals, such as hares, springhares and squirrels and even wild fruit and the odd scorpion. They are also poultry raiders.

Breeding Two to five young are born (although three is a more common number) throughout the year, but mainly in the early part of the year. The gestation period is about two months. Wild cats breed freely with domestic cats and the resulting offspring lose the red colour behind the ears.

Distribution They occur widely in Africa, from the Cape up into Arabia, and in parts of Asia and India and the Mediterranean islands.

SERVAL, ***Felis serval***
Shona: nzudzi
Ndebele: inhlozi
Other name: serval cat
Fig. 31 *Plate* 37

Features The serval looks rather like a miniature cheetah with its long legs and slender body. Unlike the much larger cheetah however, it has a relatively short tail and fairly large ears. The general colour is yellow with black spots and bars. Each ear has a very distinct white band across the back.

Habits Servals are mainly nocturnal, occurring alone or in pairs, and hiding up during the day. The presence of water, plus cover in the form of reedbeds, tall grass or scrub bush, appear to be important habitat requirements. Such conditions are common in Zimbabwe and hence the serval is a widespread species, although it does not occur in the drier areas where no surface water is available. They are present even on the fringes of Salisbury, where young are often found in mealie lands by farmers.

They prey mainly on rats and mice but will also feed on other small mammals, birds, reptiles, insects and sun-spiders. Cane rats and vlei rats, both of which occur in the serval's habitat, are frequently eaten. They will also kill unprotected poultry. They do not appear to take such large prey as the more powerful caracal.

Small prey are usually killed with a hard downward slap of the paw, as opposed to the sideways slap of the caracal. The very flexible and narrow paws are also used to hook mice and other prey out of their holes. In long grass they may quarter an area with high leaps until some small animal breaks cover and is then speedily pounced on. They have prodigious leaping powers and can bound with ease onto a two metre high fence pole.

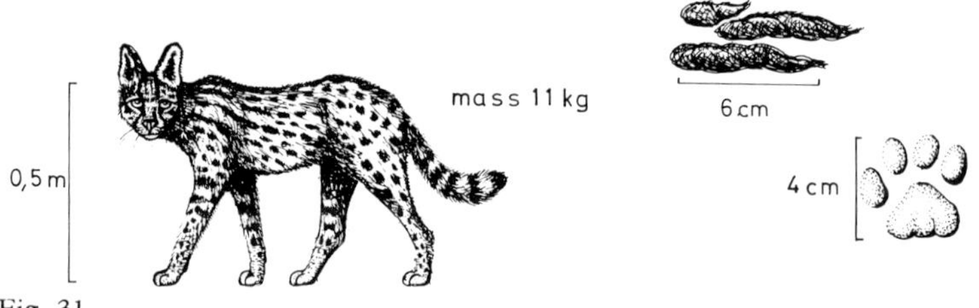

Fig. 31

Breeding From one to three kittens are born in the summer months after a gestation period of eight to ten weeks. If brought up from a very young age, they make good pets.

Distribution They have a wide distribution in Africa, from South Africa to the Sahara.

CARACAL, *Felis caracal*

Shona: hwana, twana
Ndebele: indabutshe (?), intwane (?)
Other names: rooikat, caracal lynx, African lynx, red lynx
Fig. 32 *Plate* 40

Fig. 32

Features The caracal is stockier than the serval, and is an overall reddish tan in colour, with long legs, a shortish fairly bushy tail, and long distinguishing tufts on the ears. The backs of the ears are blackish in colour.

Habits Caracals, like servals, are mainly nocturnal, solitary animals, occasionally seen during daylight hours, but normally hiding during the day in thick bush or grass where their colour blends in so well with the surroundings that they are extremely difficult to spot. Although widespread in Zimbabwe, they are not very common and hence one seldom sees them. They have a wide habitat tolerance, but require some form of cover to which they can retreat if danger threatens. They are more powerful and aggressive animals than the servals and will occasionally attack animals far heavier than themselves. Impala and reedbuck, for example, as well as the smaller antelope, are killed by caracals. The main prey animals are probably rats and mice, while dassies, hares, monkeys, springhares, reptiles and birds (including guineafowl and francolin) are also eaten. The prey is stalked in a typical cat-like manner, with a final fast rush to seize or slap down the prey with a powerful sideways strike. The prey is usually played with before being eaten. They are known killers of the smaller domestic animals such as sheep and goats.

Caracals are generally silent cats, but captive specimens purr very softly.

Breeding Normally two young are born from about September to December. Unless taken before the eyes open they are intractable animals to keep. The young are paler than the adults, and have faint spots.

Distribution They are widely distributed in Africa, although not occurring in the thick equatorial forests of west Central Africa or in the Sahara. They also occur in parts of Asia.

LEOPARD, *Panthera pardus*
Shona: mbada, ngwe/ngwe
Ndebele: ingwe
Fig. 33 *Plate* 38

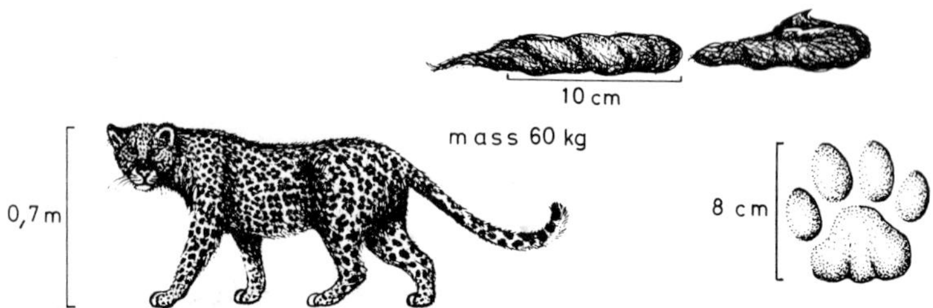

Fig. 33

Features Although the leopard rather resembles the cheetah at a distance, it is in fact more solid-bodied, with shorter, stockier legs, and a larger head. It is golden yellow in colour, with distinct black, light-centred rosettes. The cheetah has smaller, more rounded dark spots.

Habits Leopards are mainly nocturnal but may be seen during the day in areas where they are not persecuted. They occur alone or in pairs, and generally maintain a territory in which they do their hunting. They have a wide habitat tolerance and are widespread in Zimbabwe.

They eat an incredible variety of foods, a factor which enables them to live almost anywhere, even on the fringes of settlements and civilisation. In good game areas they normally eat the small to medium-sized ungulates such as impala, reedbuck, duiker, steenbuck and warthogs, but they also take larger mammals such as kudu, hartebeest and even sable antelope. In the Rhodes Matopos National Park a study showed their main items of diet were dassies, rats and mice, hares and klipspringers, but also included birds, baboons, snakes, lizards, insects, scorpions and a chameleon. In the Kruger National Park, they were recorded as eating thirty-one species of large and smaller mammals. A record exists of a leopard catching and eating bream from an island at Kariba, while in another case (in Kenya) a leopard was seen turning buffalo pats over and eating the dung beetles in them. They are also known to kill and eat the smaller carnivores, being particularly fond of baboons and dogs, and are recorded as eating putrid carrion. When natural prey is scarce they kill domestic stock and there are numerous cases in Africa of healthy leopards turning into man-eaters.

They are extremely strong for their size and often carry their prey high into trees to protect it from hyaenas and other scavengers. They may eat up to thirty kilograms of meat in twelve hours.

They frequently give voice to a harsh rasping grunt or a cough when moving about at night.

Breeding Breeding appears to be non-seasonal. Usually two to three, but up to six young are born in secluded places. The gestation period is about three to three and a half months.

Distribution They are widely distributed in Africa, from the Cape in South Africa north to the Sahara, and also occur widely in Asia. Black leopards are also known.

LION, *Panthera leo*
Shona: shumba/shumba
Ndebele: isilwane
Fig. 34 *Plate* 43

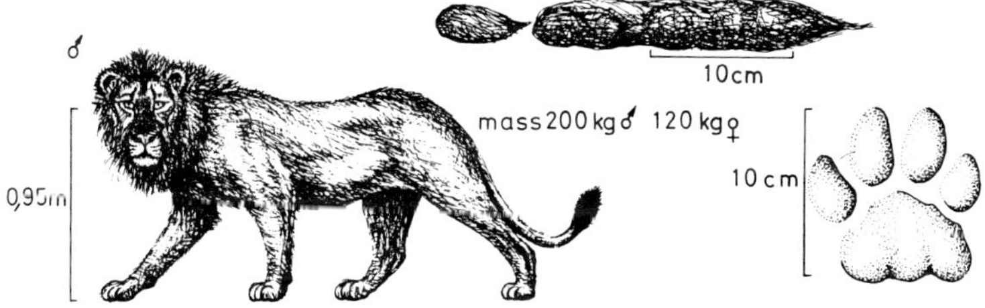

Fig. 34

Features Lions are probably the best known members of the cat family. They are usually tawny yellow, the males carrying a mane of thick hair around the neck. Females are usually lighter in colour than males. The tail has a tuft. The cubs have spots.

Habits Lions are both nocturnal and diurnal and are the only cats that can be called truly social, occurring in prides or family groups numbering up to or more than twenty individuals. These prides, however, are not completely stable and males may frequently wander off on their own, or pregnant females may leave for a while to give birth to their cubs. The size of the pride depends largely on the availability of prey and the density of cover. In East Africa, for example, where large concentrations of game occur on open plains, prides are often large, the advantage being that a kill can more effectively be made by many participants than by just a few.

Lions prey mainly on the medium-sized to large hoofed animals, usually killing whatever is most commonly available. The animals most frequently preyed upon are wildebeest, buffalo, zebra, warthog and the larger antelope such as waterbuck, impala, kudu and so on. However, they may kill virtually anything and are recorded as taking hippopotamus, rhinoceros, porcupine, ostriches and even crocodiles. They are also known to appropriate the kills of other carnivores such as hyaenas and leopards.

The lion hunts in typical cat fashion: a careful stalk followed by a quick rush to seize the animal. Several animals may participate in a hunt, thus ensuring greater success. The prey may be killed in a variety of ways. For smaller species a neck bite suffices but for larger ones the throat is often seized and strangulation follows if the actual bite does not kill. The victim may also have its nose hooked by the lion's paw, and break its neck as it falls. In the Kalahari Gemsbok National Park, lions are reported to kill gemsbok by landing on the back, digging the teeth into the haunch and jerking upwards, thus breaking the victim's back at a vulnerable spot in the vertebral column.

They drink frequently when water is available, particularly after a kill. However, they can obviously exist without it as is shown by their presence in arid parts of Botswana.

Breeding Breeding takes place throughout the year with three to four cubs normally being born. The female leaves the pride to give birth, introducing the cubs to the group when they are about ten weeks old. The cubs are weaned at about eight months but the female looks after them until they are well into their second year. During this period she does not come into heat again, and hence breeds only once in about two years. Once she has abandoned her cubs they may stay with the pride or form independent hunting groups.

Distribution Their distribution in Africa ranges from the Transvaal and parts of Zululand north to the Sahara. They also occur in one place in India.

CHEETAH, *Acinonyx jubatus*
Shona: dindingwe/dindingwe
Ndebele: ihlosi
Other names: hunting leopard, jag luiperd
Fig. 35 *Plate* 39

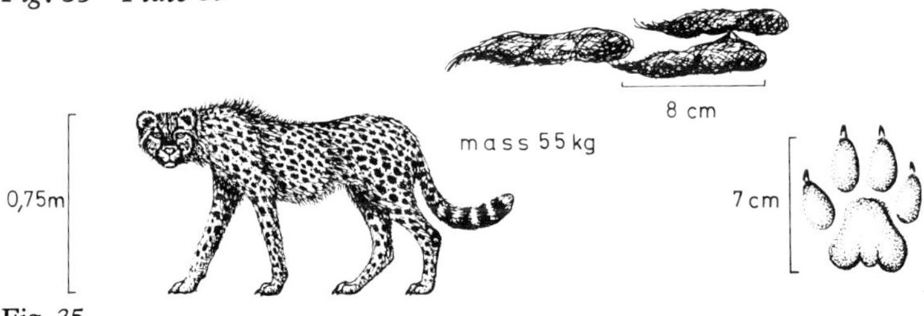

Fig. 35

Features The cheetah is a much longer, more slender animal than the leopard, with longer legs, a much smaller head, a hollow back, and characteristic black 'tear' lines from the eyes to the mouth. The claws are non-retractile, like those of a dog. The spots are much smaller and more rounded than the rosettes of the leopard. The fur is short and is an ochre yellow colour. The tail ends in a white, fairly bushy tip.

Habits In Zimbabwe, cheetahs are fairly widespread, but nowhere really common. Being shy and retiring they are seldom seen, even though they are predominantly diurnal. They are unique among the cats in that they hunt, not by stalking, stealth and pouncing, but by setting up their prey and pursuing it at great speed (up to 112 km per hour), knocking it down and then seizing it by the throat and strangling it. They maintain this speed only for about three hundred metres, after which they are completely winded and cannot undertake another chase for thirty minutes or more. They are more sociable than most cats (except lions), often occurring in groups, although usually existing as single animals or in pairs. The groups are usually either a mother with her cubs, or a group of brothers which have stuck together after the mother has left to mate again.

Adaptations for their hunting method are the non-retractile claws, required for purchase on hard ground, longitudinal ridges on the pads of the fore paws which act like tyre treads and prevent skidding, and an

Fig. 35a

extremely flexible backbone which allows the back legs to be brought far forward under the body (see Fig. 35a), giving the animal a very long stride indeed. The small (and hence light) head and deep rib-cage are also adaptations for swift movement, and the cheetah's eyesight is excellent. Unfortunately the smaller head of the cheetah means relatively smaller jaws and teeth, and therefore the cheetah experiences difficulty in killing its prey outright. Hence, its victims are generally the smaller antelope, such as impala, reedbuck, duiker and warthog, or the young of larger species such as kudu, wildebeeste, waterbuck and so on. They are known to kill larger ungulates however, particularly when two or more are hunting together. They also kill smaller animals such as hares, springhares, porcupines and guineafowl. They eat quickly, often dragging their kill into cover. When threatened they usually bluff with snarls, foot-stamping and charging, but will frequently give way.

Breeding Two to four or even five kittens are born after a gestation period of about three months.

Distribution Cheetahs have a wide distribution in Africa, occurring from Zululand northwards to Somalia and Ethiopia and then westward to Senegal. A recent estimate puts the number of cheetahs in Africa at about two thousand.

Order Tubulidentata: antbear

The antbear is the only member of this order, the name of which refers to the unique tubular structure of the cheek teeth. Some authorities regard it as being related to a primitive stock from which the hoofed mammals came. At one time the antbear was placed in a single order (Edentata) along with the other anteaters, the sloths, armadillos, and pangolins, but taxonomists decided it was not related to them and placed it in a separate order.

ANTBEAR, *Orycteropus afer*
Shona: sambani, hwiribidi/gwizo
Ndebele: isambane
Other names: aardvark, earthpig
Fig. 36 *Plate* 9

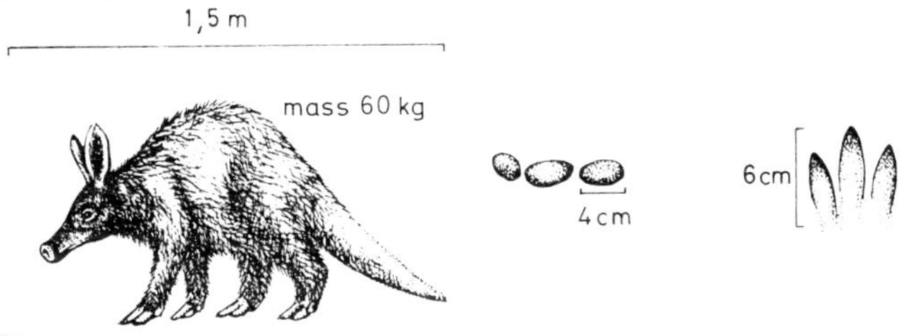

Fig. 36

Features The antbear is seldom seen because of its nocturnal habits but it may be encountered on the road at night when it will be recognised by the humped back, long pig-like snout, tall donkey-like ears and the thick tapering kangaroo-like tail. The limbs are thick and powerful, and the toes are heavily clawed (see Fig. 36a below).

Fig. 36a Foot of antbear

Habits Antbears are solitary, nocturnal animals, hiding by day in holes they have excavated and emerging at night to wander off in search of termites and ants which are their staple food. They wander long distances at night usually in a zig-zag manner and may return to their original burrow or dig another one to sleep in before daylight. They sleep curled up with the snout covered by the tail and hind feet.

Some of their burrows are fairly extensive with several passages and chambers. Inhabited burrows are sometimes revealed by the flies hovering around outside. Disused antbear burrows are of ecological importance, since they form retreats and breeding places for a number of animals, including warthogs, jackals, wild dogs, aardwolves, hyaenas, wild cats, various snakes and birds and other animals.

Antbears are often more numerous where game animals or stock are plentiful as the trampled grass and dung create favourable conditions for termites and ants. The sense of smell is highly developed and when the antbear is looking for food the nose is held close to the ground. A pause, with much sniffing of the ground, may be followed by vigorous digging.

Apart from termites and ants which are dug out of the ground or out of their nests, antbears are also known to eat beetle larvae, locusts and wild cucumber seeds. One species of wild cucumber is often found growing at the entrance of an antbear's hole. The antbear covers its droppings and the seeds contained therein are able to germinate. The fruit of this particular cucumber actually forms underground and is dug up by antbears. A record also exists of antbears eating mice.

During digging operations the ears of the antbear can be folded back so that no dirt falls in them, while dense hair around the nostrils prevents dirt and dust from entering them. The tongue can extend thirty centimetres and is whisked back and forth amongst the insects.

Breeding Antbears give birth to a single young after a gestation period of about seven months. The young antbear starts accompanying its mother a few weeks later, and starts digging when it is a few months old.

Distribution They occur throughout most of Africa south of the Sahara.

Order Proboscidea: elephants

Elephants are classified in a separate order from other mammals, as they have features not shared with any other animals.

They started evolving about sixty million years ago from a small amphibious animal no larger than a tapir. Over the next twenty million years or so evolution of the elephant progressed until mastodon, a proboscidean with enormously long tusks more than two metres long, evolved along with other elephant types. (Mastodon remains have been unearthed in the El Fayum area of Egypt.) Further evolution took place until a creature called stegodon roamed the earth. Fossil remains show that this primitive elephant had a range over the entire globe, with the exception of Australasia and South America. From it stemmed three groups: the extinct mammoth, the African elephant and the Asiatic elephant.

The mammoths were the largest proboscideans known, some standing over four metres tall. They were hunted by Stone Age man, and became extinct about twenty-five thousand years ago. The present day Asiatic elephant is the only remaining member of the Asiatic elephant group, some of which were dwarf species living on the islands of the Mediterranean.

Of the African elephant group, most are extinct, and only one species and two races, the bush elephant and the forest elephant, survive.

AFRICAN ELEPHANT, *Loxodonta africana*
Shona: nzou/zhou
Ndebele: indlovu, inkubu
Fig. 37 *Plate* 44

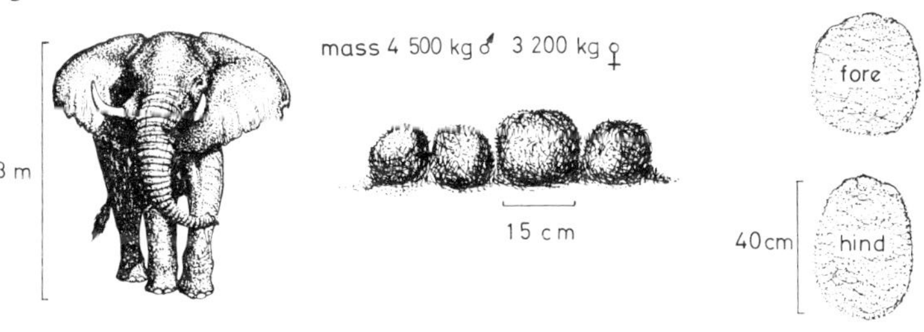

Fig. 37

Features The African elephant is the largest living land mammal, with a massive body, round pillar-like legs, a long trunk, thick skin, large ears and forward projecting tusks. Some features of the elephant are worth describing further.

The trunk, for example, is used for several purposes: gathering food, sucking up water, chastening youngsters, smelling, trumpeting, breathing, and as a weapon.

The ears, apart from being organs of hearing, have many subcutaneous blood vessels which facilitate heat loss when the elephant flaps his ears. Blood which leaves the ears is from 5° to 9° C cooler than that which enters them.

The wrinkled skin also helps in temperature regulation since it has many papilae which increase the surface area of the skin, allowing greater elimination of heat and conduction of heat by the cutaneous blood vessels.

The teeth of an elephant are decidedly unusual. The upper incisors, for example, grow forward and out to form the elephant tusks while the cheek teeth, or molars, are replaced from behind by new ones when they get worn down and drop out. Six molariform teeth develop on each side of each jaw, but never more than two of the six are in use simultaneously. The generic name *Loxodonta* means 'bow-toothed' and refers to the pattern of enamel on the surface of the cheek teeth.

The tusks of an elephant are used as weapons, as well as for digging, prising bark off trees and shaking grassy clods. An elephant may be 'right-tusked' or 'left-tusked' according to which tusk shows more wear. Generally the tusks of a male weigh from twenty-three to forty-five kilograms, while those of the female seldom weigh more than twenty kilograms.

The fore foot is slightly larger than the hind foot, although not as long. There are usually five hooved toes on each fore foot and four on each hind foot. The sole of the foot is covered with thick epithelial padding (something like crepe soles) which prevents slipping on smooth surfaces and deadens sound. The foot spreads out when the elephant stands on it and contracts when it is lifted, thus facilitating its removal from muddy ground. When an elephant walks, the legs on one side of the body move forward in unison. This is why an elephant wounded in the knee is helpless.

The elephant has no scrotum because the testes occur internally (intra-abdominal). Unlike other herbivores, the female has teats on her chest, between the front legs. Female elephants can be distinguished from males by the much more pronounced forehead (see Fig. 38).

Habits Elephants are generally gregarious animals, occurring in small to large herds, but single bulls and small bachelor herds are also

Plate 43 Lion *National Tourist Board*

Plate 44 African elephant *A. J. S. Weaving*

Plate 45 White rhino *Dale Kenmuir*

Plate 46 Bushpig *Dale Kenmuir*

Plate 47 Hippopotamus *A. J. S. Weaving*

Plate 48 Black rhino *J. M. C. Uys*

Plate 49 Warthog *Dale Kenmuir*

Plate 50 Herd of hippo *A. J. S. Weaving*

Plate 51 Steenbok *Dale Kenmuir*

Plate 52 Grysbok *Russell Williams*

Plate 53 Oribi *Michael Keep*

encountered. Formerly widespread in Zimbabwe, they are now restricted to the lowveld areas north and south of the plateau.

Despite this rather confined distribution, which has been influenced by man, elephants do in fact have a very wide habitat tolerance and, although they are large, they are very successful African mammals. Throughout most of Africa they are found in a wide variety of habitats, ranging from desert-like regions and savanna to forest and mountain-side.

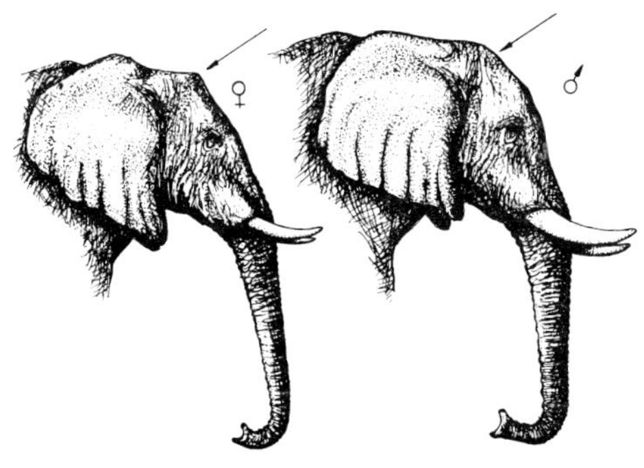

Fig. 38 Heads of male and female elephants

One of the reasons for their adaptability is the wide range of foods they are able to eat, thanks to their strength and height and the use they make of their tusks and trunk. With their strength they can shake down pods and fruit from even very large trees, while their height enables them to reach up for leaves, pods and fruit from otherwise inaccessible places. They can prise bark off trees with their tusks and with their marvellously dexterous trunk they can pluck tender shoots from the thorniest branches, reach upwards into trees for food or pluck grasses and bushes from ground level. Thus, typical elephant foods include marula fruits, mopani leaves and bark, acacia seed pods, palm fruits, grasses and a host of other vegetable foods.

Because of their enormous size and rather ineffective digestive system, they require a large quantity of food. They are therefore almost continually on the move, feeding, and resting only during the hot midday hours. Adult bulls eat between 175 and 230 kilograms of food each day, and produce an almost equally large quantity of faeces. The elephant, on average, defaecates every hour or so.

They are dependent on water, but can go for three days or so without drinking. Up to nine litres of water is sucked up by the trunk and then squirted into the mouth. Up to one hundred litres may be drunk during a visit to a waterhole. In arid areas during dry times, elephants survive by digging in river beds with their toes, tusks and trunk, and sucking up the slowly oozing water with the trunk. They are jealous of such precious water and will chase other animals away from it.

Breeding The female usually breeds during the rains when she reaches an age of about fourteen years, leaving the herd with one or two attendant cows to do so. When conditions are poor, however, maturity may be reached at a later age. One young is normally produced, although occasionally twins occur, after a gestation period of twenty-two months. The youngster weighs about 120 kg at birth and suckles with its mouth for about two years. Thereafter the female will breed about every four years. Young bulls generally leave the herd to form bachelor herds when they reach maturity, at about sixteen years of age.

Distribution They are distributed widely over Africa south of the Sahara, although absent from South Africa except in reserves. There are two distinct sub-species, the bush elephant (*africana*) and the forest elephant (*cyclotis*), which is smaller at the shoulder, has more rounded ears, and occurs in the southern Cameroons and elsewhere.

Order Hyracoidea: dassies

Dassies are interesting little mammals in that, although they look like rodents, they have affinities with the primitive stock from which elephants and sea-cows are thought to have developed. This may seem ridiculous until one considers that some of the ancestors of the dassies were as large as or larger than elephants.

They are typically small compact little mammals, similar in general appearance to guinea pigs, but larger; they are confined to Africa and parts of the Middle East. There are about nine species altogether, some of which are arboreal, while others are rock lovers.

They have some interesting features. The soles of their feet are naked and clammy (moistened by a gland), allowing them to run up almost vertical rock faces. The toes (four on the fore foot and three on the hind foot) do not have claws but small blunt nails, very like hooves. Only the inner toe of the hind foot differs in that this has a nail, modified for grooming fur (see Fig. 39a).

Fig. 39a Hind foot of dassie

On the back is the dorsal gland, which is covered by long hairs differing in colour from the general pelage. This gland probably assists dassies in identifying each other in the dark (by smell) and, when the hairs are erected, may also act as a visual alarm. Situated on the body and head are long feeler hairs (tactile hairs) which assist in keeping the animal in contact with its surroundings in the dark.

Their teeth are interesting in that the cheek teeth are very similar in pattern to those of the rhinoceros. There are only two upper incisors and these grow into sharply pointed little tusks which are capable of inflicting a nasty wound on an attacker. The lower incisors are modified to act as a fur comb. Between the incisors and cheek teeth is a gap (the diastema).

They are inquisitive and alert little creatures and can show a surprising degree of bravery and aggression in the face of an enemy.

In the Matopos, a pair of eagles takes an average of one dassie per day, and leopards prey on them extensively.

YELLOW-SPOTTED DASSIE, *Heterohyrax brucei*

Shona: mbira
Ndebele: imbila
Fig. 39 (1) *Plate* 5

Features This dassie may be distinguished from the rock dassie by its lighter coat, which is an overall grey, and the dorsal spot, which is a yellowish colour and not black as in the other species. The yellow-spotted dassie is the smaller of the two species.

Habits The habits of this species are similar to those of the rock dassie and they are found throughout Zimbabwe wherever there is suitable rocky habitat. In many places, for example Kyle National Park, the two species may be seen sunning themselves on the same rock. When this occurs the colour difference of the coat is clearly visible.

Like the rock dassies they are vegetarians, eating a variety of vegetable foods. They are arboreal to some extent. They have keen eyesight and utter shrill screams if danger threatens. Caracals, leopards, eagles and pythons prey on dassies. An eagle pair in the Matopos averages one dassie per day while predation on dassies by leopards in the Matopos is also high.

Breeding One or two young are born after a gestation period of about seven months.

Distribution Their range in Africa is not quite as extensive as that of the rock dassie and is confined mainly to the east of the continent, from the Transvaal north to Ethiopia, and also in Botswana and South West Africa.

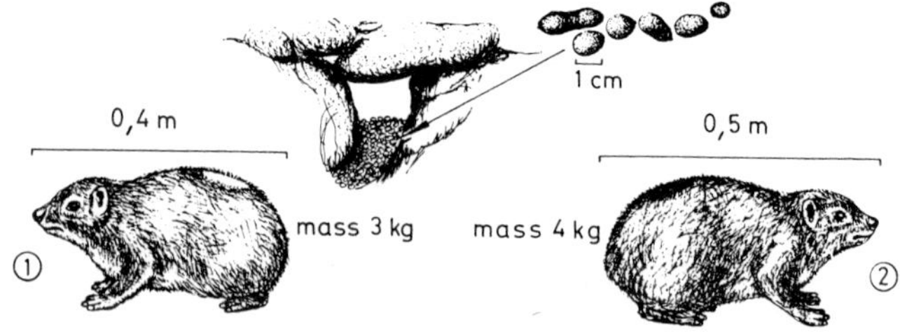

Fig. 39 (1) Yellow-spotted dassie (2) Rock dassie

ROCK DASSIE, *Procavia capensis*

Shona: mbira
Ndebele: imbila
Other names: rock-rabbit, hyrax
Fig. 39 (2) *Plate* 8

Features Where the two species of dassie occur together, the rock dassie can be distinguished by the overall brown colour, as opposed to the lighter grey of the yellow-spotted dassie. Another distinguishing feature is that the dorsal spot of the rock dassie is black, whereas in the other species it is a light colour. The rock dassie also grows to a larger size.

Habits These dassies inhabit rocky hills and kopjes where the many cracks and crannies amongst the rocks provide them with shelter from the elements and from predators. They are gregarious animals, living in small to very large colonies. Not having any natural means of defence against their enemies (such as eagles, leopards, caracals and pythons) they rely for survival on a rapid retreat to their warrens when danger threatens.

Sound plays an important part in their lives and all members are alerted to any possible danger by shrill whistles and barks. Their eyesight, which is very sharp, also plays an important part in their survival.

They have poor body temperature regulation and shelter is necessary not only for defence but to protect them from the cold and the heat. Hence on a cold day they do not appear outside, but huddle up together in their warrens for warmth. Similarly, during the hottest part of the day, they take to the shade.

They are vegetarians, feeding only for short periods in the evenings and mornings, and eating leaves, fruit, grass, bark and twigs. They will wander short distances from their rocky strongholds to feed, particularly if food is scarce.

A dassie colony is usually betrayed by urine stains on the rocks and piles of droppings in select places. Crystallised urine, 'Hyracium', is sold as a folk medicine in South Africa.

Breeding The mother gives birth to two, or sometimes three, young after a gestation period of seven months. The young are born towards the end of summer. They are able to follow the mother soon after birth.

Distribution Rock dassies occur widely in South Africa. They are also found north to East Africa, Ethiopia, Sudan, southern Egypt, and west to Algeria, Libya and the West African countries. They also occur from southern Arabia to Syria.

Order Perissodactyla: odd-toed hoofed mammals

This order has only three families, the remnants of a once large order of mammals which flourished during and after the Eocene epoch, some sixty million years ago. The present day families are the Rhinocerotidae, which contains the rhinos; the Tapiridae, which contains the tapirs; and the Equidae, which contains the horses, asses and zebras.

The ancestors of this group showed a tendency to toe reduction from five toes to the three-toed condition of rhinos and the one-toed condition of horses, an adaptation for fast movement on hard plains. The tapirs, of Asia and Central and South America, have shown least toe reduction, with four in the fore foot and three in the hind foot.

The perissodactyls did not prove to be a success, despite their widespread occurrence in the early days of mammalian history. Two of the five groups became extinct and today two groups, the tapirs and rhinos are greatly reduced, while the horses are fairly successful. There are only sixteen species left in the world today.

Zimbabwe has three species: two rhinos and one zebra.

Family Rhinocerotidae: rhinos

There are only five species. The Indian, Javan and Sumatran rhinos are found in Asia, while the black and white rhinos are found in Africa. They are all heavy-bodied, sparsely haired, thick skinned, with poor eyesight but keen hearing and scent. They have either one or two horns, made up of closely compacted fibres.

Fig. 40 White and black rhinos feeding

The two African species both occur in Zimbabwe. One of these is a browser while the other is a grazer (see Fig. 40).

BLACK RHINO, *Diceros bicornis*

Shona: chipembere, nhema
Ndebele: ubhejane
Other name: hook-lipped rhino
Fig. 41 *Plate* 48

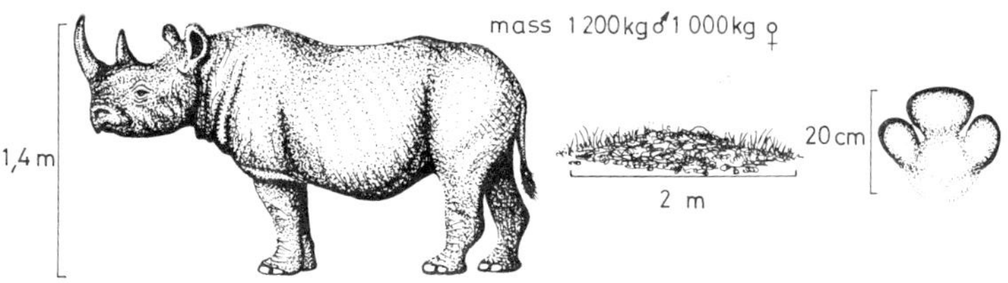

Fig. 41

Features This rhino may be distinguished from the white rhino by its smaller size, its pointed upper lip and its smaller head. The tail is carried straight up in the air when the animal runs and is not looped over the back as is the white rhino's.

Habits The black rhino is a browser and consequently it is usually found in thickets and bush country, where it eats the leaves and twigs of favoured plants, certain wild fruits, and occasionally grass. The prehensile upper lip is an adaptation for its feeding habits, enabling it to grasp and manipulate its food. The present population of Zimbabwe is estimated at less than eight hundred animals and unfortunately even these are subjected to irresponsible killing. They are confined to the Zambezi Valley, the shores of Lake Kariba, and the Sabi Valley. They have also been re-introduced to Hwange from Kariba.

They lead very solitary lives and the only really stable form of association is that between mother and calf, and this usually breaks up when the mother is about to give birth again. Males and females usually only associate for short times during the mating period.

They drink freely when water is available, but as their feeding grounds may be several kilometres away from water they can go for up to five or more days without drinking. During the hottest hours of the day they lie up in shade, conserving energy and preventing excess water loss from evaporation through their sweat glands. They enjoy wallowing in fine dust or mud, possibly to cool the skin and protect it from troublesome flies.

They defaecate in middens and also have the habit of scattering the pile with their back legs, possibly to impregnate them with scent which is then left on their paths and may serve some orientation or territory marking purpose.

They are poor sighted but have keen hearing and sense of smell and are more aggressive and temperamental than the white rhino.

Breeding There appears to be no fixed breeding season. A single young is born after a gestation period of about seventeen months. The calf may remain with the mother for a long period, following behind her as she walks.

Distribution At one time they were widespread in Africa but, because of the supposed aphrodisiac qualities of the horn, were indiscriminately slaughtered and suffered incredible reduction in numbers. Today they occur sporadically from Zululand and the eastern Transvaal north to East Africa and then west to Chad.

WHITE RHINO, *Ceratotherium simum*
Shona: chipembere, nhema
Ndebele: umhofu (?), umkhombe (Zulu)
Other name: square-lipped rhino
Fig. 42 *Plate* 45

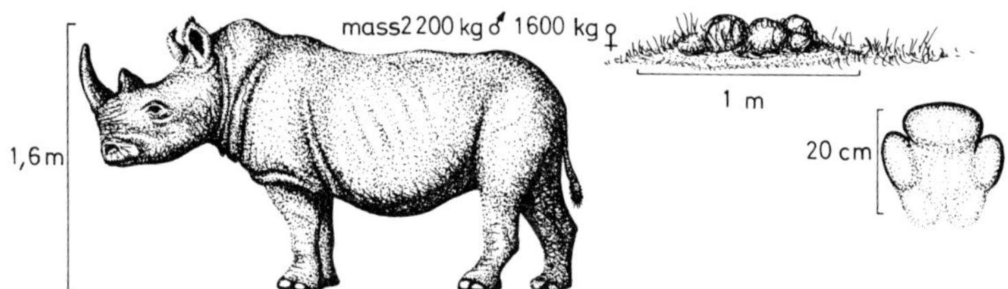

Fig. 42

Features The white rhino has a much larger and longer head than the black rhino. The upper lip is square, not pointed, and there is a prominent hump above the shoulders which is absent in the black rhino. When the white rhino runs, its tail is carried looped over its back and not straight up, as in the black rhino.

Habits White rhinos differ from black rhinos in being grazers and not browsers and consequently they have much longer heads to enable them to reach the grass. This heavier head requires greater musculature to carry it and hence white rhinos have a conspicuous 'muscly' hump between the shoulders. Another feature arising from the grazing habit is the square-lipped mouth, an adaptation for cropping grass.

They occur either solitarily, in pairs, or small family parties, feeding during the cooler hours of the day and lying up during the heat. They drink regularly and tend to deposit their droppings in middens. They are considered to be even-tempered animals, although males fight during the rutting season.

Breeding One calf is produced at intervals of about three years after a gestation period of nineteen months. The calf usually precedes the mother, whereas the black rhino's calf follows the mother.

Distribution At one time they were widespread in Africa. Unfortunately, their horns, like those of the black rhino, were prized for their supposed aphrodisiac qualities and by 1900 they had virtually been exterminated from their southern range, with appreciable numbers occurring only in Natal. Protective measures came into force, the population in Natal increased and in recent years the Natal Parks Board have exported over one thousand animals to all parts of the world, including the U.S.A., the United Kingdom, Europe, Asia and Africa. In Zimbabwe they became extinct about the turn of the century but have been re-introduced into various game reserves.

Another very small population of white rhino, considered racially distinct from ours, is found in the Sudan and Uganda.

Family Equidae: zebras

Zebras are confined to the savannas of Africa. There are three species. The largest, Grevy's zebra, has very narrow stripes and occurs north of the equator. The most southern species is the mountain zebra which occurs in mountainous areas of the eastern Cape and South West Africa, while the most common and widely distributed species is Burchell's zebra which is found from southern Africa north to the Sudan, Ethiopia and Somalia. This is the species found in Zimbabwe.

BURCHELL'S ZEBRA, *Equus burchelli*

Shona: mbizi
Ndebele: idube
Other names: Grant's or Boehm's zebra, Chapman's zebra, Selous' zebra
Fig. 43 *Plate* 42

Features The above alternative names are occasionally seen in literature on the subject and refer to sub-species or races of Burchell's zebra. This species is divided into races according to the stripe pattern on the body which varies from one region to another. An interesting feature of zebras is the shadow stripes (faint brownish stripes on the white stripes) particularly apparent on the hind-quarters. Other features are the black tufted tail, the strong upright mane, and the black patch around the nostrils.

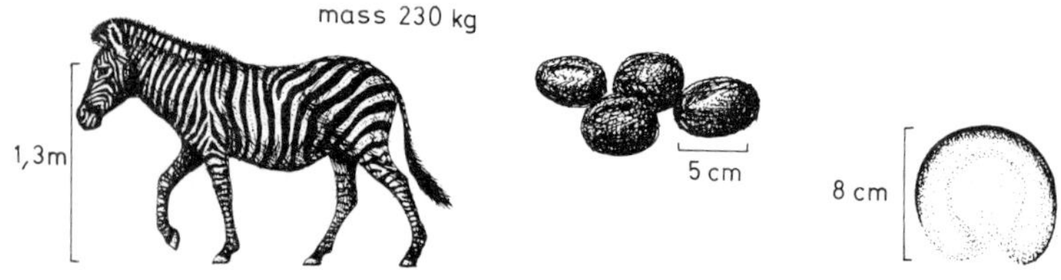

Fig. 43

Habits Being grazers, zebra are typically animals of tree and grassland savannas, often being found in association with wildebeest, hartebeest, tsessebe and other sociable species. Such loose associations are partly for survival purposes, since many heads are better than a few for spotting predators. The availability of good grazing or water may also bring species together. In Zimbabwe, zebra are found mainly in the lowveld areas, with scattered occurrences on the highveld.

Zebra are gregarious, occuring in herds numbering from a few animals up to hundreds. Such large herds are composed of family groups associating together on suitable pasture lands. More frequently, they are seen in smaller herds or single family units usually composed of a stallion and several mares and youngsters. Water and good grazing are important habitat requirements, and if either of these is lacking zebra will migrate to better areas, sometimes moving as much as forty kilometres in a night. Although primarily grazers, they are known to browse and also to dig for underground roots and rhizomes.

The longevity of zebra is probably determined by the condition of their teeth. These become increasingly worn and irregular until effective grazing is impossible and the animal rapidly loses condition and eventually dies or falls prey to predators. In the Kruger National Park, the average lifespan was found to be about twenty years. Lions are the main predators. Zebras neigh, squeal and also give a type of high pitched bark.

Breeding Single young are born from July to September after a gestation period of about twelve months. Twins are occasionally born.

Distribution They occur from Zululand north to the Sudan, Ethiopia and Somalia.

Order Artiodactyla: even-toed hoofed mammals

This group contains the greatest number of larger mammals found today, and has an almost world-wide distribution. It includes the wild pig, giraffe, antelope, buffalo and hippopotamus. The dominant feature of mammals in this order is that they rest the weight evenly on two toes of each foot, and they always have an EVEN number of toes (four or two).

Another characteristic feature, found in the vast majority of artiodactyls, is the complicated stomach which has two to four chambers; the animals which have a four-chambered stomach regurgitate their food and 'chew the cud', or ruminate. The artiodactyls with complicated stomachs are known as *ruminants*. This type of digestive system allows the animal to gather food quickly and later regurgitate and chew it in a safe and secluded place; possibly this factor has contributed largely to the success of this group in the world.

Another feature, found in all except the pigs and hippos, is the lack of upper incisors and canines, these being replaced by a hard pad against which the animal chews (see Fig. 5b). Typically the front teeth are separated from the back teeth by a gap, the *diastema*. The vast majority of even-toed hoofed mammals possess horns or antlers. Most of man's important domestic animals come from this group.

There are twenty-seven species in Zimbabwe and approximately one hundred and ninety species in the world.

Family Suidae: wild pigs

Pigs are medium-sized ungulates with stocky bodies covered with coarse hair, long heads which end in a hard rubbery snout and four toes on each foot. Only the middle toes are used for walking however,

Fig. 44 Foot of wild pig

the other two being reduced and not even touching the ground (see

Fig. 44). Both the upper and lower tusk-like canine teeth point upward. The stomach is simple and non-ruminating (that is the animals do not chew the cud), and their diet is fairly omnivorous.

There are eight species altogether, two of which are found in Zimbabwe.

WARTHOG, *Phacochoerus aethiopicus*

Shona: njiri
Ndebele: ingulube (yeganga)
Fig. 45 (1) *Plate* 49

Features Warthogs are medium-sized robust animals, sparsely haired, with barrel-like bodies, thin legs and a fairly long tufted tail which is carried stiffly erect when the animal runs. Both sexes have wart-like protuberances on the face. The tusks, particularly large in the males, are characteristic of warthogs and are in fact enlarged upper canines (see Fig. 5b). The skin colour, often determined by the colour of the mud in which they wallow, is generally grey.

Habits Warthogs are widespread in Zimbabwe although absent from high plateau areas. They usually occur as single adult males, in bachelor groups, or family groups consisting of mother and young. During the mating season males join the females.

A number of factors have allowed warthogs to compete successfully with other herbivores on the African savanna where predators abound and food is often scarce. One of these is their habit of using the holes of antbears and other animals for refuge from predators and inclement weather. Warthogs are strictly diurnal animals (although very occasionally they may feed during bright moonlight nights), taking to their holes in the evening and emerging in the morning, thus avoiding nocturnal predators. Another factor favouring their survival is their ability to root up succulent grass rhizomes with their noses during the dry season when food is scarce. Normally however, they are grazers and favour short grasses. They drink daily and enjoy wallowing in water, but their presence in arid parts of Botswana suggests they can do without surface water if necessary.

Breeding Because of the confined space of their burrows, litters are small, usually only three or four young being born from October to December, when fresh young grasses are sprouting. Mortality of the young is sometimes fairly high, but this disadvantage is offset by the fact that females breed when they are only eighteen months old. The gestation period is about four and a half months.

Distribution Warthogs are widespread in Africa, occurring from

Zululand north to the Sudan and Ethiopia and then westwards to Senegal and Mauritania.

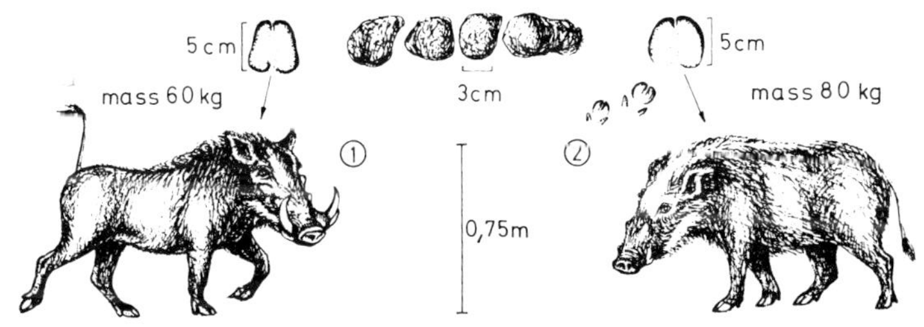

Fig. 45 (1) Warthog (2) Bushpig

BUSHPIG, *Potamochoerus porcus*

Shona: humba/nguruve
Ndebele: ingulungunda
Fig. 45 (2) *Plate* 46

Features Bushpig are variable in colour but are commonly reddish brown, typically pig-like animals. Characteristic features are the fairly long wiry coat, a dorsal crest of long white hair, black legs, a long tail and snout, and fairly large pointed ears. The male has much larger wart-like protuberances above the upper tusks than the female. This is a feature used when sexing bushpig from skulls.

Habits Bushpig are very successful African mammals in that, not only are they widely distributed over almost the whole continent south of the Sahara, but they occur even on the fringes of settled and civilised areas and are widespread in Zimbabwe.

They are successful because of their secretive nocturnal habits, their keen senses, their habit of hiding in dense thicket during the day and their rather omnivorous feeding habits. Another factor is that many of their natural enemies, mainly the large carnivores, are scarce in many areas where bushpig occur.

Like the typical forest dwelling antelope they are 'wedge-shaped', carrying the head low, and thus they are admirably adapted for dashing into and through dense thickets. Their general colouration, reddish with black and white, blends in well with the surrounding foliage and the tusks, unlike those of the warthog, are small and do not impede their progress in thick bush.

They are gregarious, occurring in parties of up to twelve or more, emerging in the evenings to feed. Although primarily vegetarians, eating roots, wild fruits and grass, they are also omnivorous and eat insects, eggs, old bones and even carrion. They can be a menace in agricultural lands, destroying the mealies and rooting up crops with their hard snouts. In the wild, however, the uprooting of hard ground allows rain to sink in to the benefit of the vegetation. They can be dangerous adversaries.

Breeding The sows give birth to litters of from three to seven piglets in nests constructed in their hideaways. Breeding takes place mainly from November to February. The gestation period is about four months.

Distribution They are widespread throughout Africa south of the Sahara except in the drier areas.

Family Hippopotamidae: hippos

Hippos are not greatly unlike members of the pig family, the differences which exist being due principally to the different habits and mode of life. For example, they have certain adaptations because they are semi-aquatic. They are similar to pigs in that they have non-ruminating stomachs (that is they do not chew the cud), stout bodies with short legs, and four toes on each foot. Unlike the pigs however, all four toes touch the ground, the two lateral toes being almost as well developed as the middle two toes. In true ungulate fashion all the toes are capped by hooves.

There are only two kinds of hippo, both confined to Africa. One of these occurs in Zimbabwe.

HIPPOPOTAMUS, *Hippopotamus amphibius*

Shona: mvuu/ngwindi
Ndebele: imvubu
Fig. 46 *Plates* 47 *and* 50

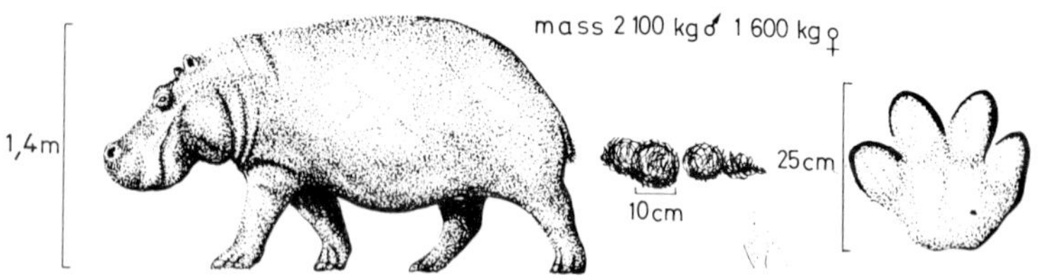

Fig. 46

Features Hippo are the only hoofed mammals in Zimbabwe which can be described as semi-aquatic. A special adaptation for their aquatic life is the positioning of the eyes, nose and ears which all protrude from the water when the rest of the animal is submerged (see Fig. 46a). The nostrils are mere slits and can close underwater, while the ears are small and unobtrusive. The lower incisors are developed as large tusks and kept sharp by the upper smaller incisors which act as 'strops' (see Fig. 5b). Both the incisors and canines are unusual in that they grow continuously.

Fig. 46a

Habits In Zimbabwe hippo are mainly confined to the water systems of the lowveld areas, occasionally occurring in the highveld. They spend most of the day in the water, either wholly or partially submerged and emerge at night or in the afternoon (if the day is cool) to graze on the banks. They are gregarious animals, occurring in mixed herds of up to twenty or more animals. Lone bulls are often encountered.

They are strictly grazers, cropping the vegetation with their wide lips and often moving several kilometres inland to find good grazing. They eat as much as forty kilograms of vegetation in a night. They can be very destructive to crops grown on river banks. A peculiar habit of the hippo is to wag its tail vigorously when defaecating, thus scattering the dung over a wide area. Possibly this is a form of territory marking or perhaps the habit arose in the water where smaller pieces of dung thus broken up would drift away in the current rather than sink as a big mass and accumulate on the river bed.

Their role in nature is a useful one. They stir up the sediments which have sunk to the bottom of the pool and thus make food and nutrients available to other organisms. They also bring nutrients from the land (where they feed) to the waters (where they defaecate, although they also defaecate on land). Their daily movements help to keep water channels and reed beds open and their broad backs provide resting places for many species of birds.

Breeding The males often fight fiercely and inflict deep wounds with their lower canines. Breeding occurs at any time of the year and the female gives birth to a single young on land after a gestation period of about eight months. The young frequently suckle under water. Females sometimes get the 'wanderlust' and move many kilometres across country in search of a suitable place to live.

Distribution They have a wide distribution in Africa, occurring from Zululand north to the Sudan and Ethiopia, and west to Gambia. The only other species is the pigmy hippo of West Africa.

Family Giraffidae: giraffes

This family also includes the okapi of Central Africa. Giraffes are peculiar animals, confined to Africa, with unusual morphological features. They are characterised by their long necks (with only seven vertebrae as in other mammals), long prehensile tongues, attractive colour pattern, long legs, relatively short bodies, and bony horns covered with fur, and not a horny sheath as in the antelope.

They are found only in Africa although related fossils are known from Greece, India and China showing that they enjoyed a much more extended range at one time. Their colour pattern varies tremendously and at one time these varieties were regarded as separate species. They are now regarded as one species, however, and the different varieties have been separated into races or sub-species.

GIRAFFE, *Giraffa camelopardalis*

Shona: furiramudenga/twiza
Ndebele: intundla/idlulamithi
Fig. 47 *Plate* 41

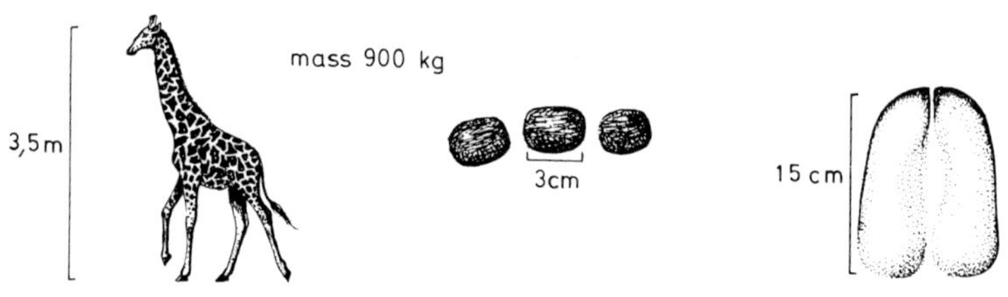

Fig. 47

Features Giraffes are the tallest of all land mammals. The males stand up to five metres high; females are smaller than the males and are lighter in colour. The markings consist of irregular-shaped brown patches separated by tawny lines. Both sexes have horns.

Habits Giraffes are gregarious animals, occurring in small herds; old bulls are often solitary. In Zimbabwe they are found only in Hwange and adjacent areas, and in the southern and south-eastern lowveld.

They feed during the day and drink regularly but are known to live for months in waterless areas. They browse on the shoots and twigs of certain trees, particularly acacia species, but occasionally graze. They have keen eyesight and good hearing and sense of smell. A popular belief is that giraffes are mute. They do in fact have vocal cords and, whether or not connected with these, utter a variety of noises including

Plate 54 Common duiker *Dale Kenmuir*

Plate 55 Blue duiker *Russell Williams*

Plate 56 Suni *Russell Williams*

Plate 57 Klipspringer *Peter Johnson*

Plate 58 Impala *Dale Kenmuir*

Plate 59 Reedbuck *Dale Kenmuir*

Plate 60 Waterbuck *A. J. S. Weaving*

Plate 61 Gemsbok *Alan Kemp*

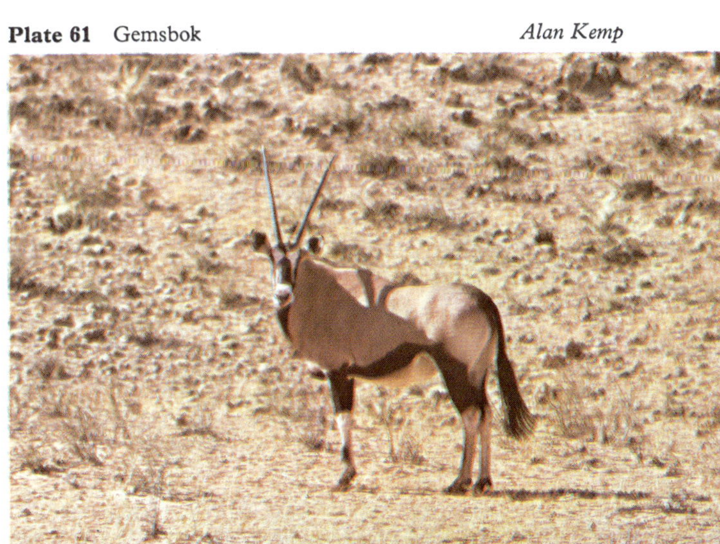

Plate 62 Roan *A. J. S. Weaving*

Plate 63 Sable *A. J. S. Weaving*

Plate 64 Tsessebe *Peter Steyn*

snorts, grunts, snores and a mooing sound. The males 'joust' by banging their heads against each other's shoulders and chest, often for long periods. Fortunately their heads are fortified by extra layers of bone. They kick powerfully in defence. In flight they are incredibly graceful and a delight to watch. Lions are their main predators.

Breeding A single young is born after a gestation period of about fifteen months and breeding takes place throughout the year. The lifespan is about twenty years.

Distribution They are found from the eastern Transvaal northwards to the Sudan and Ethiopia and west to Senegal. They also occur in Botswana, South West Africa and Angola.

Family Bovidae: antelope, buffalo

This family comprises the sheep, cattle, goats and antelope of the world. There are one hundred and ten species of which Zimbabwe has twenty-three: twenty-two antelope and one buffalo.

A characteristic of the bovids (hollow-horned animals) is the horns which, unlike those of the deer, are unbranched and never shed. They also differ from deer horns in that they are composed of a horny sheath growing around a bony core whereas the horns of deer consist of a solid bony core covered with a velvety material. Bovids are generally found in grasslands and their body form and size varies widely. The upper incisors and canines are absent (Fig. 5b), the grass being gripped between the lower incisors and canines and the upper hard pad in the top jaw (zebra have upper and lower incisors). The lower canines are shaped like the incisors to form the lower cutting teeth.

The antelope are grouped into a number of sub-families.

Sub-family Cephalophinae: duikers

These are small antelope comprising the forest duikers of which there are many species and the bush duiker of which there is one species. They are characterised by having crests or tufts of hair between the horns and distinct facial glands (pre-orbital glands). The forest duikers have hunched backs with the head carried low giving them a 'wedge' shape, an adaptation for dashing through thick undergrowth. Horns are found in both sexes in the forest duiker and only in the males in the bush duiker. There are two species of duiker in Zimbabwe: the bush duiker and the blue duiker.

BLUE DUIKER, *Cephalophus monticola*
Shona: ?
Ndebele: ?
Other name: forest duiker
Fig. 48 (1) *Plate* 55

Features This species is the smallest of all duikers. The overall colour is a grey-brown, the back being darker than the rest of the body. Both sexes have short strongly ringed horns which curve towards each other at the tips (Fig. 4a). Other characteristics are the red tinge on the front legs, white on the chin and upper throat, and a dark line from the nostrils to the top of the head.

Habits Few people have seen blue duiker because of their small size (the smallest antelope in Zimbabwe) and because they inhabit thick forest and bush where they lead very secretive lives. They are found only in the forests of the Eastern Highlands.

They are well adapted for forest life, with their very short horns, low forequarters and low hung heads which allow them to dash through the undergrowth. In addition, their greyish brown or dark slatey colour blends in well with forest shadow.

Like all forest dwelling antelope they are browsers, feeding on leaves, shoots and berries. They also drink regularly from the streams found in their habitat. They are a common prey of the crowned eagle, as well as frequently falling victim to the snares of Africans because of their habit of using regular trails.

Breeding They produce a single young at birth. The gestation period is six to seven months. Breeding takes place throughout the year with a peak in September/October. They are known to live for at least seven years.

Distribution They occur from the Cape, north through Mozambique to Kenya, in west Central Africa, and along the coastal regions of West Africa.

COMMON DUIKER, *Sylvicapra grimmia*
Shona: mhembwe
Ndebele: impunzi
Other names: grey duiker, bush duiker, Grimm's duiker
Fig. 48 (2) *Plate* 54

Features The common duiker is a small to medium-sized antelope with a rather tawny coloured coat. Distinguishing features are the black blaze on the face (nose to forehead), the black line halfway up the fore leg, the tail with black above and white below, and the conspicuous glands below the eyes on the sides of the face. Only the males carry horns (although occasional horned females are known) and these are straight and diverge at the tips (Fig. 4a).

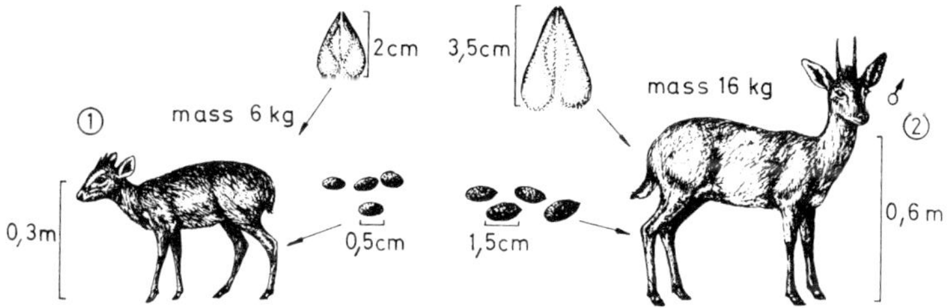

Fig. 48 (1) Blue duiker (2) Common duiker

Habits These are probably the most successful of all African antelope, being found throughout Africa, from the lowest altitudes to very high altitudes. They occur throughout Zimbabwe in a very wide variety of habitats.

Their success is undoubtedly due to their solitary and nocturnal habits, their elusive nature and, probably most important of all, their very catholic diet. For, although they are mainly browsers preferring soft green leaves and shoots, they also eat fruits, such as the duiker berry (see Fig. 48a), flowers, bark, stems, dry leaves and even underground tubers and roots which they dig up. They are also recorded as eating mopani caterpillars and guineafowl chicks. Another factor favouring their success is their independence of surface water. They have been observed to go without drinking for three years in captivity.

Fig. 48a Duiker berry

Although mainly nocturnal they also feed in the early mornings and late afternoon. They are particularly fond of cultivated lands which are usually adjacent to the cover where they can hide during the day. When disturbed they make off in a series of zig-zagging bounds, generally putting some form of cover between themselves and the source of the disturbance. If pressed they are extremely fast and have little trouble in evading a dog. Normally their brownish yellow colour blends perfectly with rank grass and scrubby bushes and makes them difficult to see.

Breeding Duiker breed throughout the year giving birth to a single young after a long gestation period. Only at mating times are the male and female together.

Distribution They occur throughout Africa although not in the thicker forest areas, as for example in west Central Africa.

Sub-family Antilopinae: steenbok, grysbok, oribi, suni, klipspringer

These are all small antelope with straight pointed horns found in the males only. They differ from duikers in lacking the crest of hair between the horns. These animals are not strongly related, the group being more one of convenience than one based on taxonomic criteria. Some authors have split them up into several sub-families.

STEENBOK, *Raphicerus campestris*
Shona: mhene
Ndebele: inqina
Other names: steinbok, steenbuck
Fig. 49 (1) *Plate* 51

Features This is a slim delicate attractive little antelope, reddish-brown in colour with a white belly. Only the males carry horns and these are black, shiny and sharp-pointed, smooth and curving slightly forward, with no rings at the base (Fig. 4a). They are frequently confused with grysbok but there are several differences. The steenbok is slightly larger, although more slender, has longer legs, longer horns and is not grizzled or flecked like the grysbok. It runs with its head high whereas the grysbok dashes away with its head low.

Habits Steenbok are usually seen alone or in pairs and are lovers of lightly wooded countryside or open grassland, provided there is sufficient cover to conceal them from enemies. They are widespread in

Zimbabwe but do not occur in the Zambezi Valley or in the Eastern Districts. They are diurnal and nocturnal and in Hwange one will frequently see them browsing on the side of the road in the early morning. They are browsers and are fairly selective, favouring particular herbs and bushes from which they pluck shoots and leaves.

Of particular interest is the fact that they use antbear holes as refuges when they are pursued. Normally, however, they run off at speed, occasionally stopping to peer over their shoulders at the cause of their fright. In this position one notices their particularly large ears.

Breeding They breed throughout the year, although mainly in summer, a single young being born after a gestation period of about five and a half months. The young conceals itself in suitable cover.

Distribution They occur throughout southern Africa, and as far north as Kenya and Tanzania.

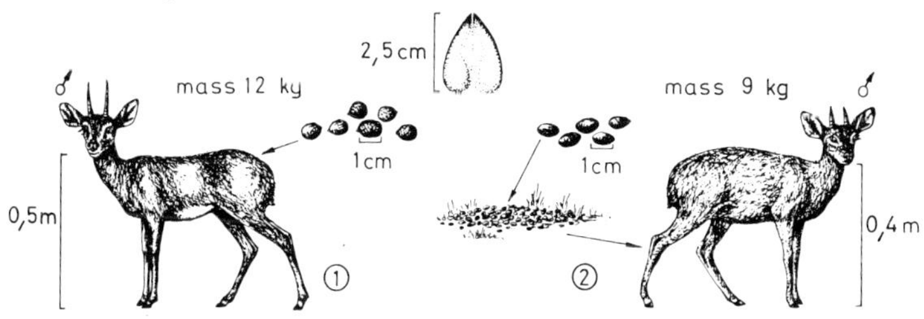

Fig. 49 (1) Steenbok (2) Grysbok

GRYSBOK, *Raphicerus sharpei*

Shona: deke/timba
Ndebele: isanempa
Other name: Sharpe's grysbok
Fig. 49 (2) *Plate* 52

Features The grysbok is slightly smaller than the steenbok and its rufous red coat is sprinkled with white hairs giving it a rather grizzled appearance, especially on the flanks. Both the tail and horns are short and the latter, found only in the males, are widely spaced, with no rings at the base (Fig. 4a). The throat has a white patch.

Habits These little antelope occur widely in Zimbabwe. They are mainly nocturnal, although diurnal to some extent, and can often be seen feeding in the late afternoon or early morning. They have a preference for stony hilly country with good cover or thick woodland and bush. Typical grysbok country is that found between Kariba and Makuti where these antelope can be seen at night, feeding on the road verges.

They are mainly browsers, eating tender leaves and young shoots, but they also graze. Their presence in an area is often betrayed by their middens; they deposit their tiny droppings in the same place. They are not easily flushed, usually breaking cover only when one is upon them. They run low and far, not pausing to stare back like the steenbok. Like steenbok however, they are known to take refuge in antbear holes when pursued.

Breeding A single young is born. Breeding takes place throughout the year, although mainly in the summer.

Distribution They are not as widely distributed in southern Africa as steenbok, occurring in the east from the Transvaal through Mozambique to Tanzania. A closely related species is the Cape grysbok (*R. melanotis*) occurring only in the Cape Province of South Africa.

ORIBI, *Ourebia ourebi*
Shona: sinza, tsinza
Ndebele: insiza (?)
Fig. 50 *Plate* 53

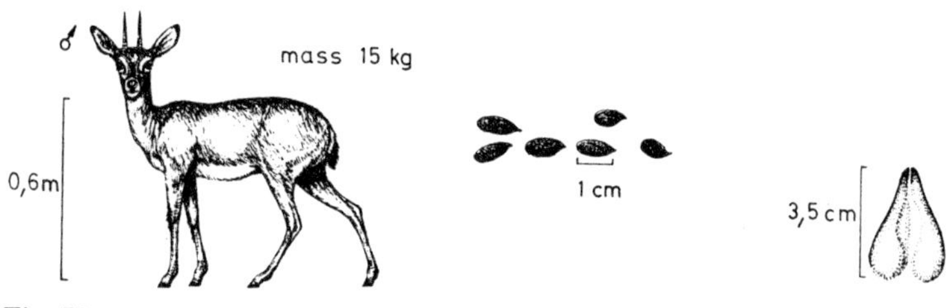

Fig. 50

Features This is the largest antelope of the Neotraginae group. Its distinguishing characteristics are its orange-red colour, a conspicuous bare glandular spot below the base of the ear, a short bushy tail with black above and white below, white underparts, and tufts of long hair on the knees. There are also small lateral or false hooves which are not found in steenbok, grysbok or common duiker. Only the males have horns, which are slender, sharp, ringed at the base, and curve slightly forward (Fig. 4a).

Habits Oribi differ from the other small antelope in being mainly grazers, and hence one finds them on grasslands, open plains, dambos, thinly bushed country and woodland savanna. They are usually found near water and, in Zimbabwe, occur mostly on the Mashonaland plateau, although they also inhabit areas in the north-west of Zimbabwe, such as the Victoria Falls region. They are not common, possibly because of their preference for open country, where they are easily seen and hunted.

Oribi are normally seen in pairs or occasionally in small groups. They rest during the day and feed in the morning and late afternoon. When fleeing, they utter a shrill whistle and bound off, jerking and pausing every so often to look back. They can move extremely fast.

Breeding Breeding takes place in the second half of the year, when a single young is born after a gestation period of about seven months.

Distribution They are fairly widely distributed in Africa although rather patchily, from eastern South Africa, north to the Sudan and Ethiopia, through Angola and Zambia and westwards to Senegal.

SUNI, *Neotragus moschatus*
Shona: ?
Ndebele: ?
Other names: Livingstone's suni, Livingstone's antelope
Fig. 51 *Plate* 56

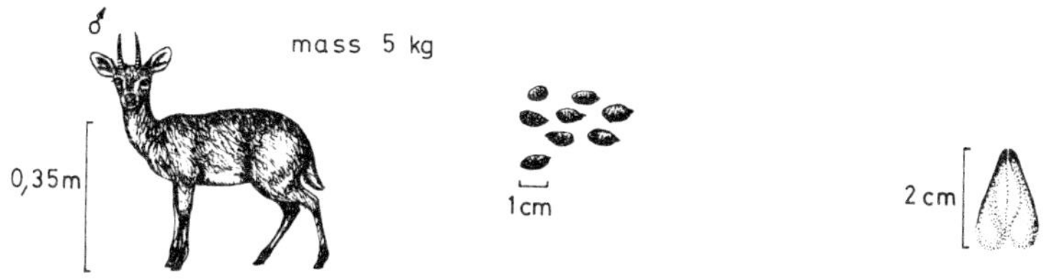

Fig. 51

Features The suni is a small antelope about the size of the blue duiker, with a reddish brown, slightly speckled coat and pure white underparts. The horns, found on males only, are heavily ringed, and directed backward to lie in the plane of the forehead (Fig. 4a). Other distinguishing features are the longish tail, which has a black line above and white below, the black ring of hair above the hooves, and the dark hair on the face.

Habits Suni have rather similar habits to blue duikers in that they frequent thick bush or forest, are usually solitary or found in pairs, and are browsers. They differ however, in that they inhabit bush in the lower lying and hotter regions occuring in the south-east lowveld and in the north and north-east of the country.

The specific name *moschatus* is said to come from the fact that they have a strong, musky smell, originating from glands below the eyes.

They feed in forest clearings in the mornings and evenings, browsing on leaves and shoots. When alarmed they utter a whistling snort.

Breeding Little is known of their breeding habits. In Natal they appear to breed from October to December.

Distribution They occur from Zululand, north through Mozambique to Kenya.

KLIPSPRINGER, *Oreotragus oreotragus*
Shona: ngururu
Ndebele: igogo
Fig. 52 *Plate* 57

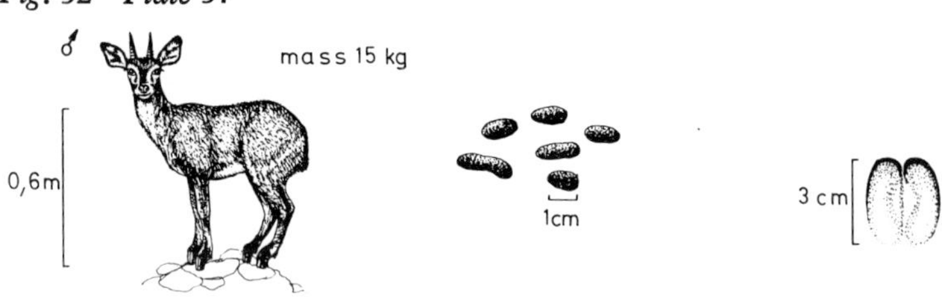

Fig. 52

Features The klipspringer is a compact little antelope with a grey-brown, rather speckled coat, a short muzzle, stumpy little tail, and black fur above the hooves. The widely spaced horns, found in males only, are ringed at the base and rise almost parallel, curving slightly forward (Fig. 4a). The hooves are small and blunt.

Habits Klipspringers are found in rocky and hilly country, and, although widespread in Zimbabwe, they are restricted to such areas. They are adapted for life on the rocks with their small cylindrical, vertically inclined hooves which can find purchase on the smallest of projections (see Fig. 52a). In addition, their greyish lichen coloured coat blends in perfectly with their rocky surroundings and, when motionless against their background, they are very difficult to see. The coat is unusual in that it is fairly springy and probably acts as a cushion against bumps and bruises from the rocks. It moults during the period September to February.

Fig. 52a Hoof of klipspringer

They are normally found in pairs or slightly larger parties and are diurnal, feeding mainly in the early mornings and later afternoon and resting during the heat of the day in the shade. They are browsers, their food including wild fruits and pods. Like the grysbok they deposit their droppings in middens, usually on flat ground amongst rocks. They characteristically stand motionless atop a large rock, their backs humped, forming a picturesque silhouette. They have definite home ranges. The alarm call is a shrill trumpet-like whistle or snort.

Breeding They breed throughout the year. A single young is born after a gestation period of about seven months.

Distribution They are distributed in Africa from the Cape northwards to Ethiopia and the Sudan. They also occur in South West Africa, Angola and northern Nigeria.

Sub-family Reduncinae: reedbuck, waterbuck

These are medium-sized to large antelope with well developed horns found only in males. The horns are strongly ringed but never twisted (as in the kudu group) and curve backwards, upward and forward (Fig. 4b). Mainly grazers, they are usually associated with water. Included in this group are the lechwe, kob and rhebucks. Zimbabwe has only two species.

REEDBUCK, *Redunca arundinum*

Shona: bimha
Ndebele: umziki
Other name: rietbok
Fig. 53 *Plate* 59

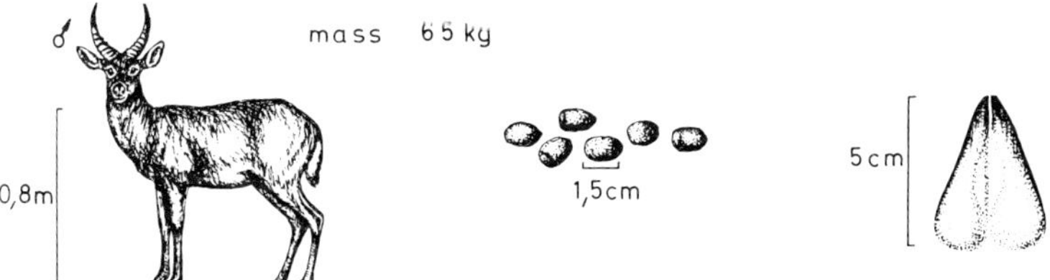

Fig. 53

Features The reedbuck is a medium to large antelope with a brownish coat tending to grey or yellow. Characteristic features are the light or white underparts, the dark stripe down the front of the legs, a bare glandular patch below the ears, and the bushy tail distinctly white underneath which 'flashes' as it bounds away. Only the males have horns and these are fairly short, curved backwards and then forward, and ringed almost to the tip (Fig. 4b).

Habits Reedbuck are widely distributed in Zimbabwe, favouring grassland or vlei, or well grassed treed areas in association with water. They do not occur in the Limpopo or Zambezi Valleys.

They are normally found singly, in pairs or threes, and very occasionally in larger groups. The males maintain a territory which they are extremely loath to leave, even when pursued, usually running in circles to remain within their home ground. They do not adapt to other types of habitat and, where bush encroachment occurs to the detriment of grass or vlei, they are likely to disappear. Unlike many of the larger antelope, they are very independent and do not associate with other species.

They are grazers, occasionally taking small herbs and browse, and are able to utilise the less palatable species of grass which other antelope tend to avoid. Thus they are not serious competitors for other grazers and are able to survive well in poor grassland if enough cover and water is available. They generally feed in the early mornings and late evenings, as well as after dark, and occasionally during the day (particularly in the dry season when feeding is extended). An interesting behavioural trait of reedbuck is 'sham drinking' or 'sham grazing', when they put their head to water or grass then suddenly lift it to look around for predators. When resting, each animal normally faces in a different direction. Although the male is dominant, the female usually leads during movements to and from feeding or drinking. When alarmed, reedbuck give a loud whistle.

Breeding Breeding is not strictly seasonal and lambs are dropped throughout the year, after a gestation period of about seven and a half months. The young conceal themselves in thick cover until they are older.

Distribution They occur from Natal northwards through Tanzania and Uganda to the southern Sudan.

WATERBUCK, *Kobus ellipsiprymnus*
Shona: dhumukwa
Ndebele: isidumuka
Other name: common waterbuck (to distinguish it from defassa waterbuck)
Fig. 54 *Plate* 60

Features This is a large greyish antelope with coarse, fairly long hair, a distinguishing and conspicuous white ring on the rump encircling the tail, and a white band on the throat. The females are slightly smaller than the males and lack the strongly ringed curving horns of the males (although occasionally a female may have small horns). A characteristic of the waterbuck is that the hair and body are very oily in comparison with other ungulates. The meat is coarse with a heavy muscle striation.

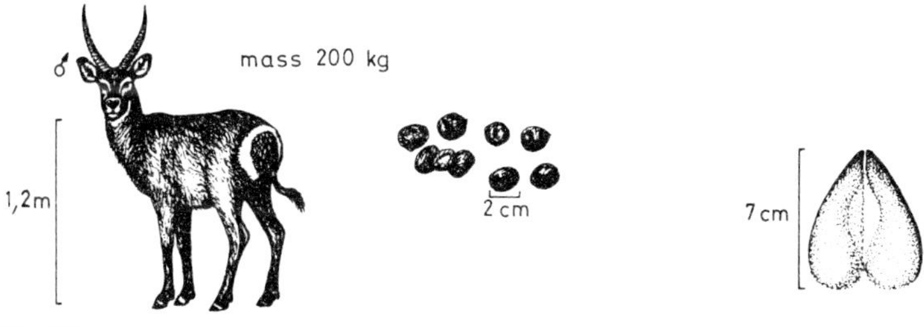

Fig. 54

Habits Waterbuck are generally gregarious antelope, occurring in herds of up to twenty, usually composed of females, young and a bull. Bachelor herds are also encountered. In Zimbabwe, waterbuck occur mainly to the north and south of the plateau (Zambezi Valley, Hwange and the southern lowveld) in tree and bush savanna and usually in association with water.

They are predominantly grazers although they are known to browse and take wild fruits. Feeding takes place mainly in the early mornings and mid-afternoons until nightfall. When pursued, waterbuck will readily take to water to elude their pursuers. Lion are their main enemies.

Breeding Breeding takes place throughout the year. Females give birth to a single young after a gestation period of about eight months. The young is hidden in thick bush or grass where it is relatively safe from predators. Observers believe the white ring on the rump is a visual sign that the young can follow in thick vegetation.

Distribution Waterbuck occur mainly to the south of the equator although their range extends north to Ethiopia. In South Africa they are found in Zululand and the eastern Transvaal. The closely related defassa waterbuck does not occur in Zimbabwe but is found in Zambia.

Sub-family Aepycerotinae: impala

Impala were formerly grouped together with the gazelles but, because of obvious differences, are now placed in a separate sub-family. Differences include the different bone structure of the skull and the fact that female impala have four teats instead of two and lack the horns that female gazelles carry. They also differ from all other antelope in that they bear two glands, covered by black patches of hair, just above the hooves of the hind legs, and they lack the false hooves that other larger antelope carry. There is only one species of impala, although the black-faced impala of South West Africa and Angola is sometimes considered to be a separate species.

IMPALA, *Aepyceros melampus*

Shona: mhara
Ndebele: impala
Fig. 55 *Plate* 58

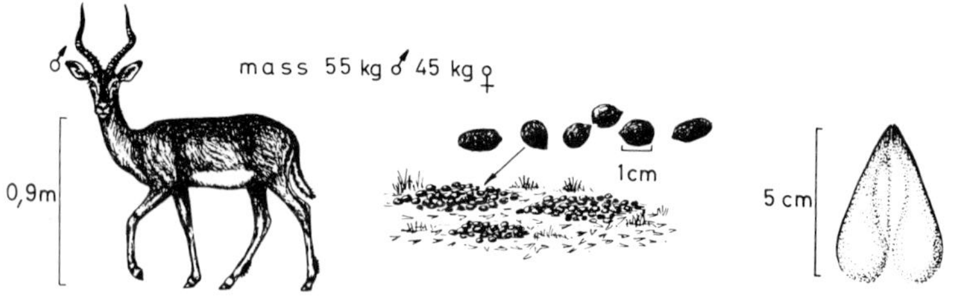

Fig. 55

Features Impala are attractive medium-sized reddish coloured antelope, differing from other large antelope in that males, females and young all have a similar colouring. In a large herd the male can usually be differentiated only by the stately horns that he carries, the females being hornless, although occasional horned females have been recorded. Distinguishing features are the black tufts of hair just above the hind hooves, white underparts, white on the throat, a fairly long tail which is usually tucked between the legs and has a white tip, and two dark vertical lines on the rump on either side of the tail (see Fig. 55a).

Fig. 55a Rump of impala

Habits Impala are well known antelope, occurring in the lowveld areas of Zimbabwe, where they favour savanna woodlands, particularly mopani. They associate in herds which can be of two types — harem herds consisting of ewes and young with a single dominant male, and bachelor herds.

Impala both browse and graze and are able to make use of a wide variety of plants. As a result, rather arid areas can support large numbers of impala, an important consideration if one is contemplating game ranching. They feed both day and night and, except when resting during the hotter hours, are usually on the move. When disturbed they give the alarm by snorting loudly and then taking off in leaps and bounds, sometimes clearing ten metres or more in one leap.

Breeding During the rut, males fight fiercely, although rarely is a contender hurt. Breeding takes place from November to January and single young are born after a gestation period of about seven months.

Distribution Impala are found in the savannas from Zululand north to Kenya and Uganda, and westwards to South West Africa and Angola.

Sub-family Hippotraginae: gemsbok, roan and sable

These are all large antelope which have well developed horns (borne by both sexes), hairy muzzles, long and tufted tails, manes of stiff and straight hair on the neck, large square teeth like those of cattle rather than antelope, and no conspicuous face glands. This group includes the addax of the Sahara (which has no mane) and the extinct blue antelope or blaauwbuck which was exterminated in the Cape in about 1800.

GEMSBOK, *Oryx gazella*

Shona: ?
Ndebele: ingugama
Other name: oryx
Fig. 56 *Plate* 61

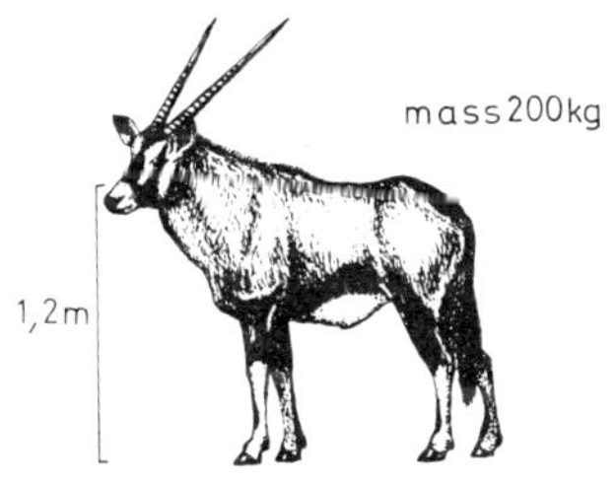

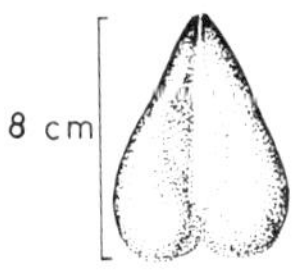

Fig. 56

Features This is the largest of all the oryxes (there are four species) and as an antelope is characterised by the very distinct and conspicuous black markings on the body and face. The coat is fawn grey while the horns are long, almost straight, and V-shaped when viewed from the front (Fig. 4b).

Habits Gemsbok are inhabitants of open plains and grassland savannas as well as semi-desert areas. In Zimbabwe they are found in the west of Hwange National Park where, like the red hartebeest, they represent an extension of the Botswana population. They also extend into the Gwaai Reserve and up to the Victoria Falls National Park.

In Zimbabwe, they occur in small herds and are mainly grazers, but they do eat wild fruits, especially melons and succulent roots and bulbs which they dig up with their fore feet. Although generally independent of water, they do drink if it is available. They feed mainly during the early mornings and late afternoons, lying up during the day.

Breeding Breeding takes place towards the end of the year. The cows give birth to single young after a gestation period of eight to nine months.

Distribution Gemsbok occur naturally only in the west of southern Africa, namely South West Africa, Angola and Botswana as well as in Zimbabwe.

ROAN, *Hippotragus equinus*

Shona: ndunguza/chengu
Ndebele: ithaka
Fig. 57 *Plate* 62

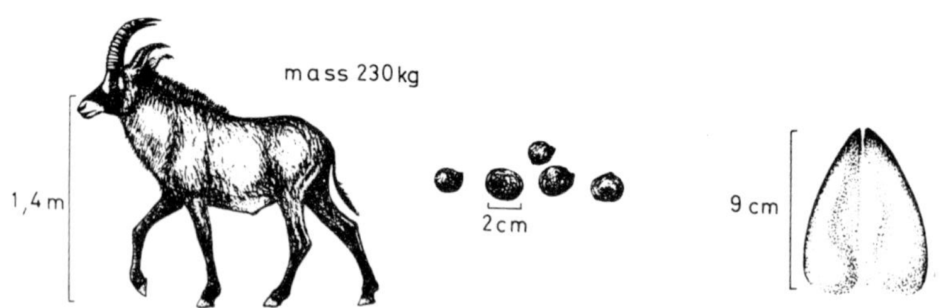

Fig. 57

Features After the eland, the roan is the largest of all antelope. It has a reddish coat with very distinct black and white facial markings and moderately long backward curving horns (Fig. 4b). The female is similar to the male but the horns are smaller. The long ears have quite noticeable tufts of dark hair at the tips.

Habits Roan inhabit wooded and grassed country with an apparent preference for a lightly wooded habitat. They are absent from most of the central watershed in Zimbabwe but occur both north and south of it. They are gregarious but are seldom found in large herds, and old bulls are often found alone. These herds are inclined to wander, according to the season, in search of food and water.

Like the sable and gemsbok they are grazers but they also take a certain amount of browse. They are particularly partial to the young green grass sprouting on burnt areas. They are seldom found far from water.

They have a reputation for being high spirited and courageous, and are dangerous opponents when wounded.

Breeding Breeding takes place throughout the year and a single young is born after a gestation period of nine months. The calf is concealed in suitable cover for up to a month after birth.

Distribution Their distribution in Africa extends from the Transvaal north to the Sudan and then east to Senegal, and from Angola east through Zaire to Tanzania.

SABLE, *Hippotragus niger*
Shona: mharapara/ngwarati
Ndebele: ingwaladi, umtshwayeli
Fig. 58 *Plate* 63

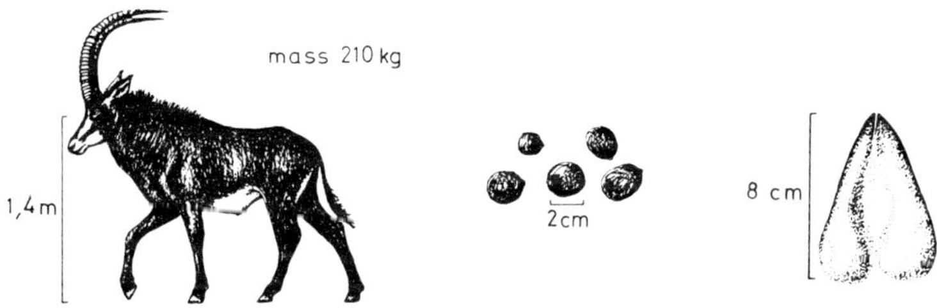

Fig. 58

Features The sable bull rivals the kudu bull as the most magnificent of all antelope. The colour is a deep and glossy brown, almost pitch black in old males, with distinctly contrasting white belly and white markings on the face. As with other members of this group, both sexes carry horns, those of the male being longer and curled back in a graceful manner (Fig. 4b). The young animals are chestnut in colour, turning darker with age.

Habits Sable associate in herds, varying from a few up to fifty or more. A herd, usually led by a cow, contains females, young and sub-adults, and on occasions an adult male. Bulls are often solitary or associate in small bachelor herds. They inhabit woodland, grassland, and often broken and fairly rugged country. They occur almost throughout Zimbabwe.

Like the roan they are grazers but are known to browse to a limited extent. At Lake Kariba they often graze on the lush grass growing on the lake shore. They are dependent on water and in fact are often found in vlei areas.

Amongst hunters they are famous for the magnificent trophies they yield (horns up to 1,3 metres) and their pugnacity when wounded.

Breeding Breeding takes place throughout the year with, in Zimbabwe, a distinct calving peak in February. A single young is born after a gestation period of about nine months. The young remain hidden for two to four weeks after birth.

Distribution Sable are found from the Transvaal to South West Africa and Angola, and north to Kenya and Tanzania. Their distribution involves three races, the most magnificent being the giant sable of Angola.

Sub-family Alcelaphinae: hartebeest, tsessebe, wildebeest

These are all large antelope. They are characterised by their long narrow faces (particularly the hartebeest), their shoulders being higher than their haunches, and the fact that both sexes have horns which are usually rather complicated, bending in different directions throughout the length and, in some of the hartebeest, arising from a horny pedicle set in the crown of the skull. All are gregarious and inhabit open country. There are nine species of which four occur in Zimbabwe.

LICHTENSTEIN'S HARTEBEEST, *Alcelaphus lichtensteini*

Shona: hwiranondo
Ndebele: inhlezu (?)
Fig. 59 (1) *Plate* 65

Features This species is slightly smaller than the red hartebeest and has a tawny or dull yellow coat with a reddish back. There is no blaze on the face as in the red hartebeest and their horns are not so high as the pedicle is much smaller (Fig. 4a). The tail is black and the front of the fore and hind legs have a black stripe. The female is similar to the male but paler and with less robust horns.

Habits In Zimbabwe they are confined to an area in the south-east

Plate 65 Lichtenstein's hartebeest *John Hanks*

Plate 66 Red hartebeest *A. J. S. Weaving*

Plate 67 Blue wildebeest *A. J. S. Weaving*

Plate 68 Nyala bull
A. J. S. Weaving

Plate 69 Sitatunga bull
Barnaby's Picture Library

Plate 70 Nyala cow *Alan Kemp*

Plate 71 Sitatunga cow *Barnaby's Picture Library*

Plate 72 Buffalo *A. J. S. Weaving*

Plate 73 Kudu *Dale Kenmuir*

Plate 74 Eland *Dale Kenmuir*

Plate 75 Bushbuck *Dale Kenmuir*

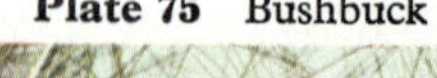

near the Sabi and Lundi rivers. Their occurrence in Zimbabwe represents the southern limit of their distribution. There is evidence that the species was far more widespread in earlier days. Following a survey which indicated that the total population in Zimbabwe probably did not exceed two hundred, seventy were introduced from Gorongosa in Mozambique to the lowveld, where they are doing well and producing calves. They prefer fairly open grassland or well grassed open woodland, and they are gregarious, usually occurring in herds of up to ten animals. Lone bulls and bachelor herds are encountered. They often join up with other animals, such as wildebeest or impala, for the greater safety found in numbers.

They are mainly grazers although they are known to eat leaves and wild fruit, and they feed both day and night. They drink daily, usually in the mornings.

The males maintain territories and fighting takes place in the rutting season. Males are said to mark their territories with secretions from the well developed pre-orbital glands. When danger threatens they have a habit of mounting anthills to have a good look around. Like the red hartebeest they are fast and enduring antelope.

Breeding Single calves are dropped before the rains with a peak occurring around August. The gestation period is about eight months.

Distribution They occur from the Transvaal in South Africa north to Tanzania. They are far more common in Zambia than they are in Zimbabwe.

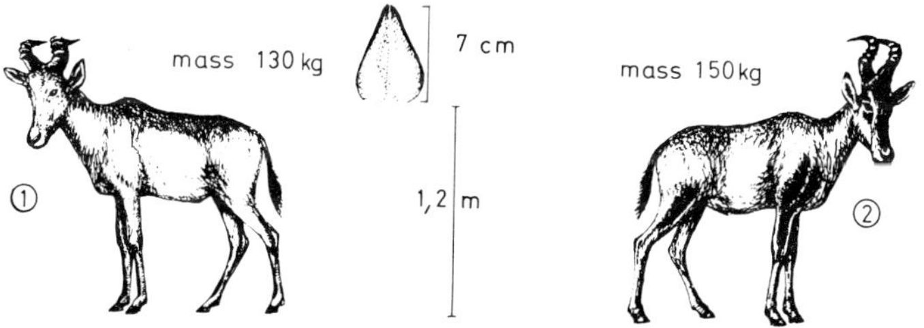

Fig. 59 (1) Lichtenstein's hartebeest (2) Red hartebeest

RED HARTEBEEST, *Alcelaphus buselaphus*

Shona: ngama
Ndebele: indluzele (?)
Fig. 59 (2) *Plate* 66

Features This species differs from other hartebeest in the much greater size of the frontal pedicle from which the horns, thick and heavily ringed, grow (Fig. 4a). The sexes are very similar, but the bulls are stouter and have larger horns. They are red or reddish brown in colour, with distinguishing darker hair on the fronts of the legs, shoulders, face and back of the neck. The upper hindquarters are much lighter, tending to a fawn colour.

Habits Their range in Zimbabwe is interesting in that it is confined to the extreme south-west corner of the Hwange National Park. Their occurrence there is an extension of their fairly widespread distribution in Botswana and represents the north-eastern extension of red hartebeest found on the Makgadikgadi grasslands of Botswana. They are wanderers and occasionally turn up in the south-east of Hwange and in the Plumtree area. They have also been seen in the Inyati area.

They occur in fairly small herds in Zimbabwe, although in Botswana herds are large, numbering up to three hundred animals. They are almost entirely grazers and are able to survive for long periods without surface water. Despite their awkward shape they are swift of foot and have great stamina; they are reputed to be able to outrun a good horse.

Breeding A single young is born, usually towards the end of the year, after a gestation period of eight months.

Distribution They occur in South Africa, South West Africa, Botswana, Angola and Zimbabwe, and then again in East Africa west to Senegal. Some authorities regard the northern hartebeest as a separate species.

TSESSEBE, *Damaliscus lunatus*
Shona: nondo
Ndebele: inkolomi
Other names: sassaby, bastard hartebeest
Fig. 60 *Plate* 64

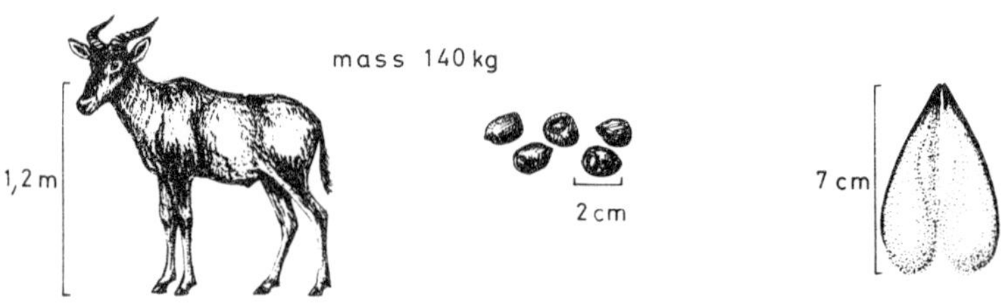

Fig. 60

Features Tsessebe are not as ungainly as hartebeest. They have simpler horns, not arising from a pedicle (see Fig 4a), and have shorter faces than the true hartebeest. The bontebok and blesbok of South Africa are related to the tsessebe. Their coat is fairly unusual in that it is a dark plum colour with a purplish gloss or sheen.

Habits In Zimbabwe, tsessebe are found in localised areas, both north and south of the plateau, where there is suitable habitat consisting of grassland, vlei and open woodland. They occur in small breeding herds of up to fifteen, and larger bachelor herds of up to twenty-five.

They are grazers, particularly fond of the succulent young grass in freshly burnt areas. They drink regularly when water is available and may, in fact, be dependent on it. Like so many of the species that prefer an open habitat, they frequently associate with other animals, including zebra and wildebeest. They are reputed to be the fastest of all hoofed mammals, capable of keeping up their fascinating bouncing gait for long distances.

Breeding They breed in the dry months preceding the rains, mainly from September to November. A single young is born after a gestation period of about eight months.

Distribution They are mainly confined to southern Africa where they occur in South Africa, west to Angola and South West Africa, and also north to Tanzania.

BLUE WILDEBEEST, *Connochaetes taurinus*
Shona: mvumba/ngongoni
Ndebele: inkonkoni
Other name: brindled gnu
Fig. 61 *Plate* 67

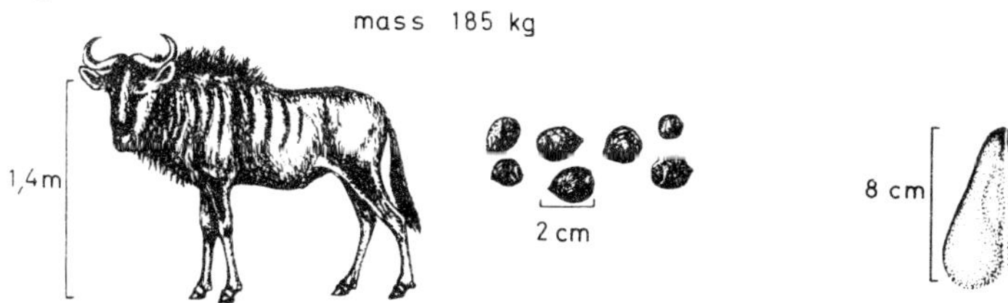

Fig. 61

Features The name 'brindled gnu' comes from the brindled appearance given to the animal by vertical lines against the generally slate grey hide on the neck and flanks. The long black hair on the head and neck together with the stocky body, spindly legs and long horse-like tail give it an unmistakeable appearance — ferocious and yet comic. The blue wildebeest is a larger animal than the South African black wildebeest. Its horns (Fig. 4a) are similar to those of the buffalo.

Habits Wildebeest are gregarious animals of grasslands or wooded grasslands, occurring in herds of up to and more than one hundred animals. In Zimbabwe they are confined mainly to the Hwange region and the lowveld and do not occur in the Zambezi Valley. They can be great wanderers, especially during hard times, and will migrate in large herds to seek new pastures. The present population of Hwange is derived from migrating herds which moved into the game park in 1934 when a drought forced them out of Botswana; although the majority returned to Botswana, a remnant remains in the park. They are mainly grazers with a distinct preference for short green grass. They drink frequently but can survive several days without water.

Although bachelor herds and mixed breeding herds are the two main herd types, single bulls are often encountered. These bulls establish a territory which they are very reluctant to leave.

Breeding Breeding takes place mainly from November to January, when new grass is available for the young. A single young is born after a gestation period of about nine months.

Distribution They occur from Zululand north to Kenya and west to Angola and South West Africa. Those in Kenya are regarded as a different sub-species.

Sub-family Bovinae: bushbuck, nyala, kudu, sisatunga, eland

These are medium-sized to large antelope with spirally twisted horns which are never ringed and, with the exception of the eland and bongo, are found in males only. A characteristic mane or crest of hair is found on the spine and the majority have spots or stripes, or both, on the body. They are generally found in an enclosed habitat. Zimbabwe has five species. Buffalo are included in this group as well.

BUSHBUCK, *Tragelaphus scriptus*

Shona: dzoma/soma
Ndebele: imbabala
Fig. 62 *Plate* 75

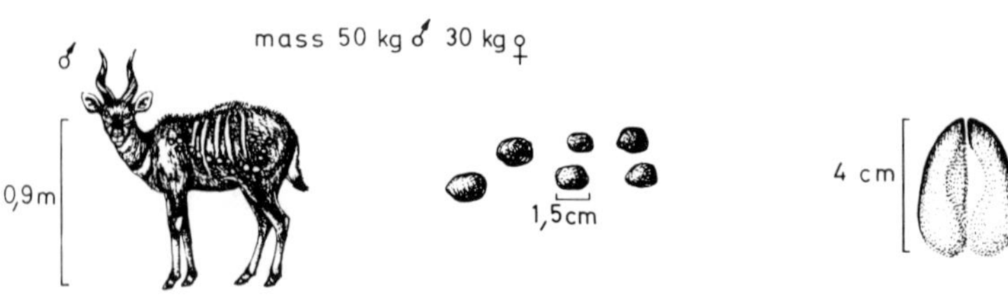

Fig. 62

Features Bushbuck are medium-sized antelope. The males are larger than the females, and are red-brown with white stripes on the back and white spots on the shoulders, hindquarters and face. The spots look like patches of sunlight and serve a useful camouflage purpose. The male has a white dorsal crest and rather short spiralled and sharply pointed horns (Fig. 4b). The female is hornless and has less conspicuous markings.

Habits Bushbuck are widespread in Zimbabwe, but restricted to areas where their natural habitat, thick bush or riverine forest, occurs. They are generally found singly or in pairs, or occasionally in family groups. They are mainly nocturnal browsers. They do not wander far from their home range, finding enough food in small areas to maintain themselves. During the heat of the day they lie up in the shade of the undergrowth, emerging in the evenings, mornings, or at night to feed. When disturbed they utter a loud bark, and if wounded they can be very dangerous.

Breeding They breed throughout the year, reaching a peak during the late rains. They produce a single young after a gestation period of six to seven months.

Distribution They occur widely in Africa from the Sahara southwards to the Cape Province in South Africa. The colour variation from area to area is quite great and many different races have been described.

NYALA, *Tragelaphus angasi*
Shona: nyara
Ndebele: inyala (Zulu)
Fig. 63 *Plates* 68 *and* 70

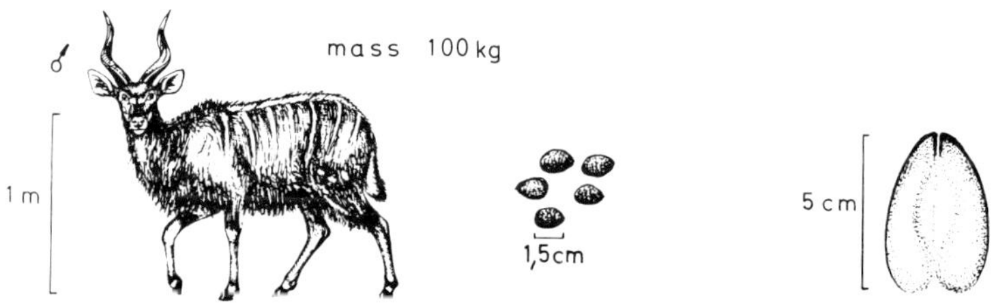

Fig. 63

Features These are handsome antelope which look rather like kudu. The male is quite different from the female and is characterised by a greyish shaggy coat with a white crest on the back stretching from shoulder to tail, and further shaggy hair on the neck, belly and rump. The horns, found in males only, are similar to those of the kudu, and have a distinctive white tip (Fig. 4b). The females are not as hairy and have a redder coat with very distinct stripes on the flanks.

Habits Nyala are unlikely to be seen by many people as they are confined to two small areas in the north-east and south-east of Zimbabwe. They have also been recorded at Mana Pools. They have been introduced to Kyle where, because of their preference for thick bush, they are not easily seen. Although they are often found near water, they are not dependent on it.

Unlike bushbuck, nyala are gregarious, occurring in small parties as do the larger kudu. Their food is predominantly browse, although they do graze. They are both diurnal and nocturnal, tending to the latter where there is much disturbance. They have a bark similar to that of the bushbuck and, like that animal, can be dangerous when wounded.

Breeding A single young is born after a gestation period of eight to nine months. In South Africa there is a peak calving period from about August to October.

Distribution Nyala occur only in southern Africa, extending from Natal north to Mozambique and Malawi.

SITATUNGA, *Tragelaphus spekei*

Shona: ?
Ndebele: inzuza (?)
Fig. 64 *Plates* 69 *and* 71

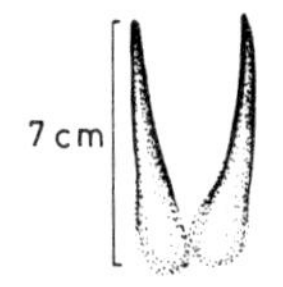

Fig. 64

Features Sitatunga are greyish brown antelope, larger and of a more slender build than bushbuck, and with less conspicuous spots and stripes. The most characteristic feature is the hooves, which are long, narrow, and widely separated at the tips. Unlike the kudu and nyala there is no dorsal mane. The horns, found on bulls only, are longer and more twisted than those of the bushbuck, and have whitish tips. Females are smaller and brown or chestnut coloured.

Habits In Zimbabwe, sitatunga are an extremely marginal species, apparently occurring only above the Victoria Falls on the Zambezi in the reedbeds of the river.

The long narrow hooves which splay out are an adaptation for walking on soft marshy ground and swamp vegetation, a habitat to which they are almost entirely restricted. In Lake Victoria, however, they are known to inhabit an island where there is no swamp and only bush, so obviously they can exist outside this habitat if they are not molested.

Shy and retiring, they generally occur singly, in pairs, or in slightly larger aggregations. If alarmed they steal away into the vegetation, or else they take to the water where they are strong swimmers. They may also dash off in a series of plunging leaps, and then stand still until danger passes.

They feed on the young shoots of reeds, sedges and grasses, and are active at night as well as during the day, often emerging during the night to feed on the margins of their habitat. The alarm call is a bark as well as a snort.

Breeding Little is known of the breeding habits of sitatunga. Single young are born, possibly throughout the year. Young animals are dark, well spotted and striped.

Distribution They are found from northern South West Africa and the Okavango in Botswana, north through Zambia and Zaire to Gambia in West Africa, and east to Uganda, Kenya and Tanzania.

KUDU, *Tragelaphus strepsiceros*
Shona: nhoro
Ndebele: ibhalabhala
Other name: greater kudu
Fig. 65 *Plate* 73

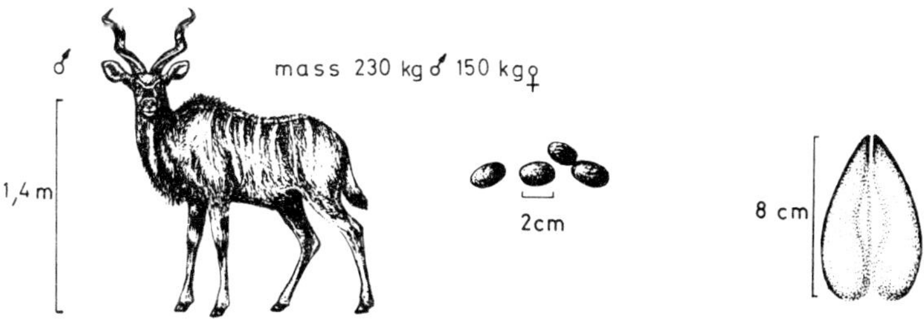

Fig. 65

Features Kudu are generally brown to grey with the males carrying magnificent spiral horns (Fig. 4b) and the females being hornless, although horned females have been recorded. They are not as hairy as the nyala, but nevertheless the males have a fairly heavy mane on the neck down to the tail and another on the throat and neck. Both males and females have vertical white bands on the sides. The males have a very distinct white bar between the eyes.

Habits Kudu are widespread but localised in Zimbabwe, as they are invariably found in broken country where there is good covering of bush or scrub. They are gregarious, occurring in small herds, usually consisting of several cows and a bull, or cows and calves. Bachelor herds are not uncommon. The older bulls often live apart, joining the cows only during the rutting season.

They are browsers, eating leaves, stems, pods and wild fruit, and also raiding crops when these are available. High fences are usually no effective deterrent to kudu. Their wariness and keen senses allow them to live in bush, even on the fringes of human habitation. Where disturbance is great they become strictly nocturnal, lying up in cover during the day and emerging to feed at night. Otherwise they feed and drink during the day. Typically they have a loud warning bark when danger threatens. When facing an intruder the large ears are turned well forward to catch the slightest sound.

Breeding Breeding takes place mainly from January to March. A single young is born, after a gestation period of about seven months. Calves suckle for about six months.

Distribution The kudu is found from South Africa, north to Somalia and Ethiopia and west to Chad. A closely related species is the lesser kudu, found only in the Kenya, Somalia and Ethiopia region.

ELAND, *Taurotragus oryx*
Shona: mhofu
Ndebele: impofu
Fig. 66 *Plate* 74

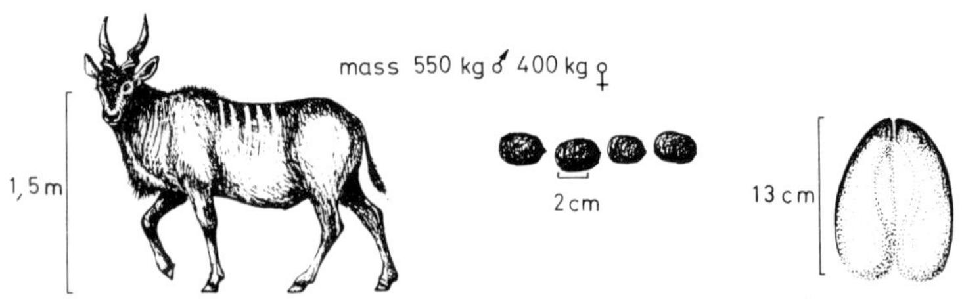

Fig. 66

Features These are the largest of all antelope. The overall colour is a light tawny brown, the flanks bearing white stripes which are more conspicuous in younger animals. Males and females are very similar in appearance, although the males are larger, turn darker with age and are distinguished by the prominent dewlap on the throat, a noticeable shoulder hump, and a large blackish tuft of bushy hair on the forehead. Both sexes carry short spiralled horns (Fig. 4b).

Habits Eland are generally found in areas of savanna woodland and scrub where they occur in herds of up to one hundred animals. They were formerly widespread in Zimbabwe but are now absent from many areas. F. C. Selous, for example, notes in his diary, '. . . I have often seen large herds numbering one hundred to one hundred and fifty individuals feeding on the present site of Salisbury.'

They are mainly browsers although they will graze. Research in Zimbabwe has shown that they may eat fifty or more different plant species and hence can survive well in areas which are not suitable for cattle. A characteristic feature of their feeding behaviour is for them to hook branches down with their horns to reach leaves which would otherwise be inaccessible.

They are important antelope in that they are easily domesticated and research has been going on since the early 1960s to evaluate their full potential as meat producers. The meat is of excellent quality and unlike most game meat carries quantities of fat. Another important consideration for domestication is that despite their large size they are docile, good natured animals.

Breeding They breed from July to November, producing a single young after a gestation period of about eight and a half months.

Distribution Eland occur from South Africa north through Mozambique to Kenya and the southern Sudan, and then west to Chad and Senegal.

BUFFALO, *Syncerus caffer*
Shona: nyati
Ndebele: inyathi
Other name: Cape buffalo
Fig. 67 *Plate* 72

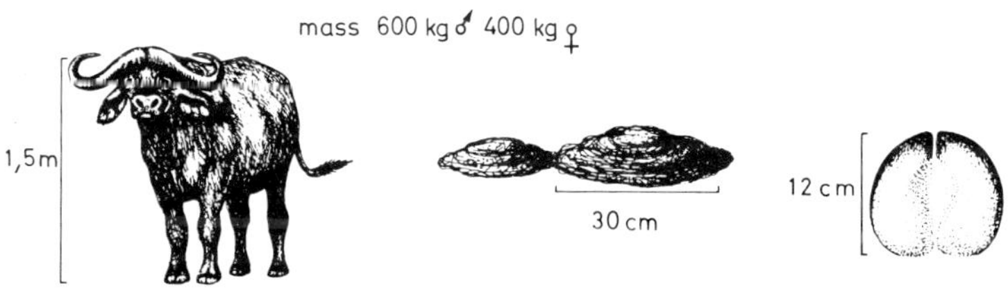

Fig. 67

Features The buffalo is a heavily built animal with a robust body, strong limbs, a long and tufted tail, thick hide sparsely covered with hair, and a broad wet muzzle. The large head is surmounted by curving black horns, found in both sexes. In the adult males the horn bases extend to the centre of the skull.

Habits Buffalo are adaptable animals. They occur in both the north and south lowveld, and inhabit quite a wide range of localities although favouring areas of woodland and vlei, with thick cover for concealment during the day.

They are mainly grazers, emerging in the cooler afternoons to feed and drink, and feeding into the night and again in the morning. Although lone bulls are frequently encountered they are gregarious animals and herds often number several hundred animals. As a game species they have always presented a challenge to big-game hunters in that, apart from yielding a magnificent trophy, they are extremely dangerous animals when wounded and display both fearlessness and cunning to the extent of deliberately lying in wait for their opponent — often with disastrous results for the hunter. Lions are their main enemies. They rely largely on their sense of smell to detect the presence of men although their hearing is good and they pick up movement well with their eyes.

Breeding The main calving season is during the dry months when single young are born after a gestation period of about eleven months.

Distribution Buffalo are widespread throughout Africa. They show distinct differences in size, colour and horn formation from area to area. Another buffalo, the dwarf forest buffalo, occurs in Central and West Africa.

Order Lagomorpha: hares

Rabbits and hares were at one time placed in the same order as rodents, but distinct differences between rodents on the one hand and hares and rabbits on the other caused zoologists to place them in two different orders.

Rodents, for example, have only a single pair of upper incisors whereas rabbits and hares have two pairs. Furthermore, the incisors of rodents have enamel on the outside only whereas those of the lagomorphs are completely covered with enamel. Blood tests have also indicated differences between the two groups, and further differences are to be found in the skeleton and in certain other features.

Rabbits differ from hares in that their young (leverets) are born naked and blind and virtually helpless whereas the young of hares are born with fur and open eyes and are fairly active soon after birth. Hares have very long hind legs and ears which are longer than the head, whereas in rabbits the hind feet are not so long and the ears are shorter than the head. Other differences are found in the skull bones. Some of the rabbits associate in groups whereas hares are usually solitary and do not burrow as some rabbits do.

Typically hares have long hind legs adapted for jumping and running, long ears, short tails and fairly short coats. They are usually solitary animals, hiding during the day and emerging in the evenings to feed. They have many enemies and, since they lack defensive means, rely on their keen sense of hearing and smell to detect danger, either lying low until it passes or depending on their swift jinking run to escape.

Zimbabwe has three species of hares belonging to the family Leporidae.

CAPE HARE, *Lepus capensis*
Shona: tsuro/shuro
Ndebele: umvundla
Fig. 68 (1)

Features The Cape hare is very similar to the scrub hare and in the field it is impossible to distinguish between them. The Cape hare is smaller however, has relatively shorter ears and is greyish on the back of the neck instead of reddish, as in the scrub hare. However, like the scrub hare, the longish tail is black on top and white below.

Habits Cape hares prefer a more open habitat than do scrub hares and are more likely to be found in areas of open grassland than in the scrub bush habitat favoured by the scrub hare. Like the scrub hare they are nocturnal, lying up during the day, often in very scanty cover where they are difficult to see. Thus they rely largely on their cryptic colouration for protection, but will dart away at high speed if flushed.

It is interesting to note that in Botswana the Cape hares found in the Makgadikgadi area, where the sand is white, are much lighter in colour than those found elsewhere. This emphasises the fact that the hare's ability to survive depends largely on its coat blending in with the natural background, thus making it difficult to see. The coat will thus vary in colour according to the habitat.

Breeding They normally occur singly, although during mating one or more males may join a female. Breeding takes place throughout the year with two young usually being born.

Distribution The Cape hare is widely distributed in Africa and, like the scrub hare, also extends into Europe and Asia.

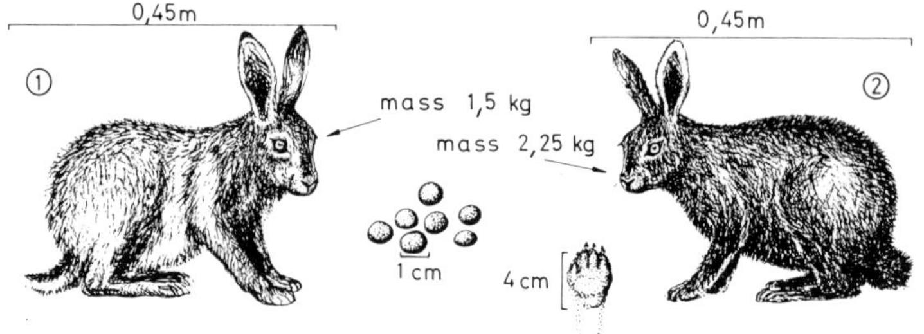

Fig. 68 (1) Cape hare and scrub hare (2) Red rock hare

SCRUB HARE, *Lepus saxatilis*
Shona: tsuro/shuro
Ndebele: umvundla
Other name: southern bush hare
Fig. 68 (1) *Plate* 76

Features In the field it is impossible to distinguish this hare from the closely related Cape hare. The general colour is grey, with white on the chest and belly and on the undersurface of the tail. The top of the tail is black and the ears and hind legs are long. The scrub hare is larger than the Cape hare, has relatively longer ears and lacks the yellowish line where the dorsal and ventral colours meet along the side, which the Cape hare has.

Habits These hares are widely distributed in Zimbabwe and are associated with scrub bush in which they hide during the day. They emerge at night to feed on surrounding grasslands and cultivated lands or gardens, where they can do quite a lot of damage.

Like most hares, they are not easily flushed from their refuges during the day and dash off only at the last moment from under one's feet. They are fast and elusive, running in a jinking manner to escape pursuers. On an open road they frequently get killed by cars as they tend to run along the road in the car's headlights, rather than escape into the bush.

Breeding The young are born throughout the year in thick cover, after a gestation period of about a month. Up to three young are born and these are soon capable of fending for themselves.

Distribution They are widely distributed in Africa and also extend into Europe and Asia.

RED ROCK HARE, *Pronolagus crassicaudatus*
Shona: tsuro/shuro
Ndebele: umvundla
Fig. 68 (2) *Plate* 77

Features Key distinguishing features of this hare are the red fur on the legs, and the reddish and very bushy pom-pom tail (in the other two species the tail is longer and coloured black and white). In addition, the back legs of this hare are shorter than those of the other two species, and are black underneath. The overall colour is a darkish grey and the coat is woolly and thick.

Habits Red rock hares are found in a rocky and hilly habitat and hence it is not surprising to find they are very common in the Matopos. They are unlikely to be seen often, if at all, however, as they are nocturnal, emerging after dark to feed and hiding during the day in rocky crevices and cracks. Their presence in an area can be shown by their droppings which are deposited in middens. The dung is composed of the dry and digested remains of grass which is their main item of food.

In the Matopos, red rock hares, along with dassies, are the principal food of leopards. When startled, they utter rather loud and startling screams as they race away. They also scream rather horribly when wounded.

Breeding Little is known of the breeding of this species. Usually two young are born.

Distribution Outside Zimbabwe they occur in South Africa and

South West Africa and then north up to the eastern part of the continent to Kenya.

Order Rodentia: rodents

Rodents are the most numerous and widespread of all mammals. There are over one thousand seven hundred known species and, in fact, two out of every five mammals on earth are rodents.

Rodents are distinguished by having a single pair of incisors in each jaw, and a gap, the diastema, between these teeth and the grinding cheek teeth or molars. A characteristic of the incisors is that they grow throughout life and hence have to be continually worn down by gnawing, otherwise they would grow too long to be used or, as they are curved, grow back into the animals mouth and cause death. Another feature of these teeth is that the outer surface, being coated with enamel, is much harder than the inner, with the result that greater wear takes place on the inner surface and the teeth assume a chisel-like or cutting shape, enabling the hardest surfaces to be gnawed.

Another interesting feature of rodents is that when they are gnawing the lower jaw moves forward and the cheek teeth do not meet, and hence will not be worn out. Also, in some rodents, the back part of the mouth is separated from the front part when gnawing, by the drawing in of the cheeks in the diastema region, and therefore chips and flakes of teeth, broken off by gnawing activities, cannot fall into the mouth and choke the animal. When the animal wishes to chew, the lower jaw moves back and the cheek teeth become operational.

Rodents occupy a variety of habitats and have assumed a diversity of forms. Some are long and slender and dwell in trees, like the squirrels, while others are burrowers and adapted for an underground life, like the mole rats. Some have enlarged hindlegs, like the springhares, and are prodigious leapers, while others, like the beavers, spend much of their life in water. While the vast majority of rodents are small animals, a few, like the porcupine and capybara, have attained the size of small pigs.

They are adaptable, resourceful and often cunning and many have combined these traits with a high fecundity which enables them to survive in the most unlikely places and often in the face of intense persecution. They cannot go unnoticed by man since some carry disease (rats), others depredate food stores and crops (rats, porcupines, springhares), others yield valuable furs (chinchillas, beavers), while others are edible and valuable as food (porcupine, cane rat, guinea pig and many rats).

Zimbabwe has thirty-eight known species of rodents, classified within seven families. These are Bathyergidae (mole rats), Hystricidae (porcupine), Octodontidae (cane rats), Sciuridae (squirrels), Pedetidae (springhare), Muscardinidae (dormice) and Muridae and Cricetidae (rats and mice). Twenty-eight of the thirty-eight species are rats and mice.

Family Bathyergidae: mole rats

Shona: nhuta, nhimbe/nhukutsa
Ndebele: imvukuzane
Fig. 69 *Plate* 81

Fig. 69 MOLE RAT

Members of this family are exclusively African in their distribution, and they are usually referred to as African mole rats (as opposed to the mole rats of other parts of the world). They are adapted for a subterranean existence. Unlike the golden moles which are insectivorous, mole rats are vegetarians, feeding on roots, tubers, bulbs and so on which they find by burrowing tunnels under the surface of the soil. They also differ from golden moles in the way that they excavate their tunnels. Golden moles break up the soil with their hard noses whereas the mole rats break it up with their very large protruding incisors.

Characteristic features of mole rats are the conspicuous incisors, very small eyes and ears, a very stubby tail, and short legs with large fore and hind feet which have naked soles and five clawed toes on each foot.

There are two sub-species in Zimbabwe. One is the damara mole rat (*Cryptomys hottentotus damarensis*) and the other is the Mashona mole rat (*C. h. darlingi*).

The damara mole rat is larger than the Mashona species and is found in sandy soil in the western parts of Zimbabwe. Its colour is blackish grey with brown tinges in some specimens, and there is a large irregular white patch on the back of the head.

The Mashona mole rat occurs in the Mashonaland region and is a fairly drab greyish colour. It has a triangular white patch on the crown. The fur is soft and silky.

Plate 76 Scrub hare *J. Anderson*

Plate 77 Red rock hare *Dale Kenmuir*

Plate 78 Springhare *W. T. Miller*

Plate 79 Porcupine *E. L. Button*

Plate 80 Giant rat *Russell Williams*

Plate 81 Mole rat *Peter Johnson*

Plate 82 Rat *Dale Kenmuir*

Plate 83 Mouse *Dale Kenmuir*

Plate 84 Sand rat *Dale Kenmuir*

Plate 85 Bush squirrel *Dale Kenmuir*

Plate 86 Red squirrel *Dale Kenmuir*

Plate 87 Sun squirrel *E. L. Button*

Family Thryonomidae: cane rats

Shona: tsenzi/senzi
Ndebele: ivondo, ibuzi (?)
Fig. 70

Fig. 70 Cane rat

Cane rats are not rats at all but are in fact more closely related to porcupines than to rats and mice. They are large, very robust rodents, with short legs and a short rat-like tail which is covered with coarse rather bristly hairs. They inhabit thick vegetation, generally near water, and they can swim and dive well. Distinct 'runs' are formed in the vegetation in areas where they live. They are vegetarian, feeding on grasses, sedges, reeds, crops and so on. Cane rats in fact are well known for the damage they can do to crops, particularly sugar cane. They generally occur singly or in pairs. From two to four young are born. Africans are particularly fond of eating these large rodents.

There are two species in Zimbabwe: the greater cane rat (illustrated above) (*Thryonomus swinderianus*) and the lesser cane rat (*Thryonomus gregorianus*). The greater cane rat is widely distributed in Africa from South Africa to Senegal, whereas the lesser cane rat has a more limited distribution, occurring from Chad and the Sudan to Zimbabwe.

Family Muscardinidae: dormice

Fig. 71

Fig. 71

These are small animals which look rather like miniature squirrels but which have a mouse-like anatomy. They are found only in Europe, Asia and Africa.

Characteristic features are the bushy tails (which distinguish them from rats and mice), soft fur and large eyes. They have short curved claws adapted for climbing trees and rocks.

Dormice are mainly nocturnal rodents with a fairly omnivorous diet consisting of vegetable foods, seeds and some insects. In the colder climates dormice hibernate during the cold weather (hence 'dormice' from the French *dormir*, meaning to sleep). The edible dormouse of Europe was much favoured by the Romans as a table delicacy.

Two species are found in Zimbabwe, *Graphiurus murinus*, simply called dormouse, a forest or arboreal dormouse; and *G. platyops*, the rock dormouse (see Fig. 71). The forest dormice are small forms with rather plain colouration. The species here is nocturnal and arboreal, resting in holes in trees or roofs during the day.

The rock dormouse is fairly large and has a broad flat skull which allows it to squeeze into rock crevices.

Family Muridae and Cricetidae: rats, mice

Rat—Shona: gonzo
Ndebele: igundwane
Mouse—Shona: mbeva
Ndebele: igundwane
Giant rat—Shona: mhunzamatura/dapi
Ndebele: ?
Plates 80, 82, 83 *and* 84

This family contains the rats and mice. They are small rodents which have bodies usually covered with fur, and tails which may be furred, naked or scaley and vary tremendously in length. They are mainly terrestrial, some burrowing and others being arboreal, and they are generally nocturnal, although some are diurnal. The large forms are commonly called rats and the small forms called mice, there being no clear distinction between the two. Some examples of Zimbabwean rats and mice are shown in Fig. 73.

The sand rats, or gerbils, differ from the rest in that they leap, kangaroo-like, on their long hind legs, and use their tail, which is often tufted, as a counter-balance. They also commonly hoard food and live in burrows, generally in the drier parts (Plate 84).

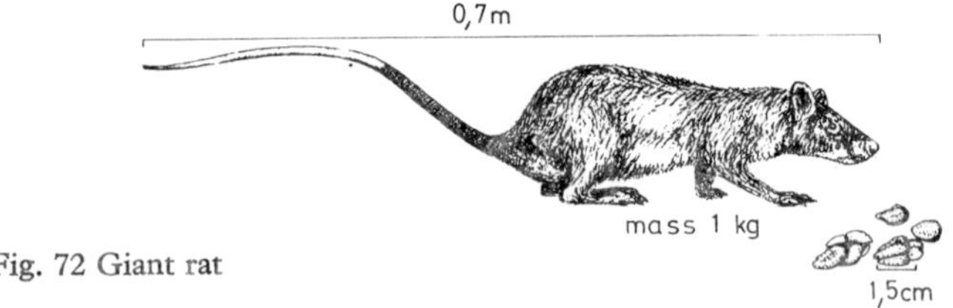

Fig. 72 Giant rat

Zimbabwean rats Included in these families is the largest rat known,

Fig. 73 Some examples of rats and mice

Cricetomys gambianus, the giant rat (Plate 80). This animal is unique in that it carries parasitic cockroaches. Other more common rats and mice found in Zimbabwe are the Namaqua rock mouse (*Aethomys namaquensis*), which commonly lives in a grassy nest amongst rocks; the four-striped mouse (*Rhabdomys pumilio*), a diurnal species that one often sees up at Inyanga; the multimammate mouse (*Praomys natalensis*), which breeds prolifically, has up to twenty mammae and is commonly found in cultivated areas; and the red veld rat (*Aethomys chrysophilus*), a species preferring to inhabit thick grass.

Other interesting species are the pouched mouse (*Saccostomus campestris*), which has a short tail and large cheek pouches; the arboreal forest mouse (*Thamnomys dolichurus*), with its very long tail; the house rat (*Rattus rattus*—introduced), also known as the black rat, probably originated from Asia, well known because it carries a flea which spreads the plague; the house mouse (*Mus musculus* — introduced), commonly found living in houses in association with man, and originally from the dry areas of Europe and Asia; the single-striped mouse (*Lemniscomys griselda*), belonging to a genus of diurnal mice which are widespread in Africa; the spiny mouse (*Acomys spinosissimus*), an interesting mouse in that the fur of the back and tail has been modified to form coarse spines; the creek rat (*Pelomys fallax*), a medium-sized rat with black markings on the rump; the vlei rat, angoni vlei rat and large vlei rat (*Otomys irroratus*, *Otomys angoniensis*, *Otomys maximus*) found in damp vlei areas; the fat mouse and the small fat mouse (*Steatomys pratensis*, *S. minutus*) with fat little bodies and short tails; the grey pygmy climbing mouse and the lesser climbing mouse (*Dendromus melanotis*, *D. mystacalis*), which are both climbing mice; the minute pygmy mouse (*Mus minutoides*); the water rat (*Dasymys incomtus*); the black-tailed tree rat (*Thallomys paedulcus*); and Rudd's rat (*Uranomys ruddi*).

Finally there are the species of gerbils, or sand rats; the lesser gerbil (*Gerbillurus paeba*); the Gorongoza gerbil (*Tatera inclusa*); Brant's gerbil (*Tetara brantsi*) and Peter's gerbil (*Tatera leucogaster*).

A total of twenty-eight species of rats and mice, some of which are illustrated in Fig. 73, have so far been recorded in Zimbabwe.

Family Hystricidae: porcupines

There are two types of porcupines: the smaller brush-tailed porcupine belonging to the genus Atherurus, and the larger common or crested porcupines belonging to the genus Hystrix.

There are several species of crested porcupines occurring in Africa, Europe and Asia. Only one species inhabits southern Africa however, and this is the one found in Zimbabwe.

PORCUPINE, *Hystrix africaeaustralis*

Shona: nungu/chinungu
Ndebele: inungu
Fig. 74 *Plate* 79

Features The porcupine is the largest and probably the best known African rodent, characterised by the spines and quills which cover the back and tail and which serve as a means of self defence. The eyes are fairly small, and the legs short and thick.

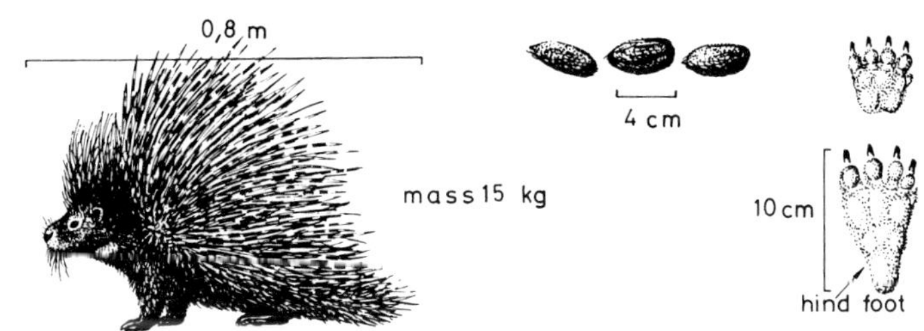

Fig. 74

Habits Despite their size and conspicuous form they are successful animals with a wide habitat tolerance; they are widespread and common in Zimbabwe. They owe their survival to their habits of moving about and feeding at night (usually noisily), and hiding during the day in old antbear holes, caves, rock crevices and burrows which they dig themselves. Their presence in these places is often betrayed by quills lying about on the ground outside. They occur singly, in pairs, or in small parties, occupying a communal retreat.

Another factor contributing to their survival is the defensive coat of quills they carry. If molested, the porcupine erects these and rattles them in a very intimidatory manner; and if this fails to deter the enemy the porcupine will rush backwards and attempt to stab the attacker. The quills are never shot out at the enemy, but if they are pushed in, they come away easily, leaving themselves embedded in the molester. Despite this defensive armament, the larger predators occasionally kill porcupines, although they seldom emerge unscathed from the attack. Many Africans also favour them as food, as the meat is very palatable.

Like other rodents, porcupines have a typically varied vegetarian diet, which includes roots, bulbs, wild fruits, berries, bark and cultivated crops such as groundnuts, melons, maize, potatoes and so on. They are often hunted at night by crop farmers with spotlamps, dogs and guns. They are also known to chew old bones, a habit which keeps the incisors worn down to a manageable level.

Breeding From one to three young are born from July to December.

Distribution This species occurs from South Africa northwards to Tanzania.

Family Sciuridae: squirrels

The squirrel family has an almost world-wide distribution. Most are tree dwellers but some, like the ground squirrel, marmots and chipmunks, are ground dwellers. This family also includes flying squirrels, woodchucks and prairie dogs. Zimbabwe has three species, all of which are tree dwellers, with typical squirrel features; long slender bodies, bushy tails, short limbs and small ears lying close to the head. Tree squirrels are found only in wooded country or in dense forest.

SUN SQUIRREL, *Heliosciurus rufobrachium*
Shona: shindi
Ndebele: ubuhlula
Other name: red-legged sun squirrel
Fig. 75 (1) *Plate* 87

Features This is a slightly larger squirrel than the bush squirrel, having rather similar coloration, but occurring only in the east of Zimbabwe in montane evergreen forest where the bush squirrel does not occur. Its tail is ringed and it has a red or orange tinge on the legs, hence the alternative name.

Habits Sun squirrels have similar habits to bush squirrels, being diurnal, nesting in holes in trees, and eating a variety of vegetable foods, including fruits, berries and young leaves.

As with many of the smaller species living in forests, little is known about them. There are about ten species of sun squirrels, occurring northwards from Zimbabwe to Ethiopia and westwards to Gambia. They also occur in Angola and Mozambique. The colour of this particular species (*H. rufobrachium*) varies a great deal from one area to another, and, while it may be light coloured in one area, it will be dark in another. Even in Zimbabwe the colour appears to vary from season to season.

Breeding They generally produce from one to three, or even five, young in their tree holes from about June to October.

Distribution Zimbabwe is the southernmost limit of its distribution, which extends northwards to Ethiopia and also westwards to Angola and Gambia.

BUSH SQUIRREL, *Paraxerus cepapi*
Shona: tsindi/shindi
Ndebele: ubusinti
Other names: mopani squirrel, yellow-footed squirrel
Fig. 75 (2) *Plate* 85

Features This is the small brownish yellow squirrel which occurs widely throughout Zimbabwe wherever there is suitable woodland habitat. It cannot be confused with the rather similar looking sun squirrel as this species occurs only in montane and evergreen forest in the Eastern Districts where the bush squirrel is absent. The latter is particularly common in mopani woodlands.

Habits Bush squirrels are strictly diurnal and occur singly, in pairs or in family groups. They live in holes in trees which is one reason why they are so common in mopani woodland as these trees are riddled with holes.

They feed on a wide variety of vegetable matter, foraging both in trees and on the ground. Their diet includes leaves, wild fruits, seed pods, flowers and even grass. Insects, such as beetles and cicadas, are also eaten. They become exceedingly tame when living close to humans and respond readily to being fed, being very partial to peanuts. They have an amusing habit of storing food away in any convenient crack or crevice when one feeds them, and peanuts and sunflower seeds turn up in the most unlikely places.

When they become annoyed or excited they chatter vigorously, frisking the tail up and down and facing the source of the annoyance in a most aggressive manner. If they cannot escape to their holes they hide very effectively behind branches and leaves. They retire to their holes well before sundown and emerge after sunrise, when they are prone to sunbathing.

Breeding It appears that they may breed throughout the year, but mainly during summer. Usually two young are born but occasionally three.

Distribution This species occurs from the Transvaal north to Ethiopia.

RED SQUIRREL, *Paraxerus palliatus*

Shona: ?
Ndebele: indlegu
Fig. 75 (3) *Plate* 86

Features This little squirrel, about the size of the bush squirrel

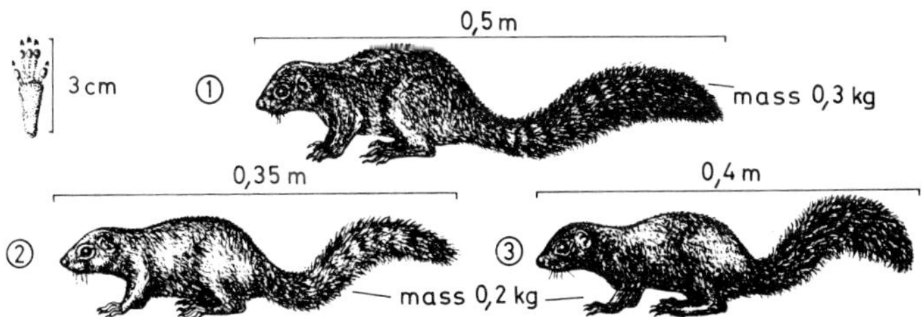

Fig. 75 (1) Sun squirrel (2) Bush squirrel (3) Red squirrel

derives its name from the bright red and very attractive fur on the underparts of the body and on the tail and legs. The upper parts are rather dark.

Habits These squirrels live in the Mount Selinda forest where they inhabit thick undergrowth and forage on the ground for food. They are diurnal and seen in pairs. Very little is known about their habits. Although reputed to be vegetarian, a tame animal at Kariba ate grasshoppers and moths with gusto, and it is probable that insects figure largely in their diet in the wild. This animal also ate peanuts, sunflower seeds, flowers and other vegetable matter, and spent a lot of time foraging on the ground, generally near cover. Quite often it would cling from a branch with its back legs only, while examining something interesting with its front feet. This animal was strictly diurnal, retiring for the whole night to a nest in the ceiling that it made itself.

Breeding One or two young are born.

Distribution Ranges from Zululand northwards along the eastern half of Africa through Mozambique to Tanzania.

Family Pedetidae: springhare

The springhare has no close relationship with any other group of rodents and hence is placed in a group of its own. There is only the one species, confined to Africa.

SPRINGHARE, *Pedetes capensis*
Shona: nhire, gwidzu
Ndebele: umahelane
Fig. 76 *Plate* 78

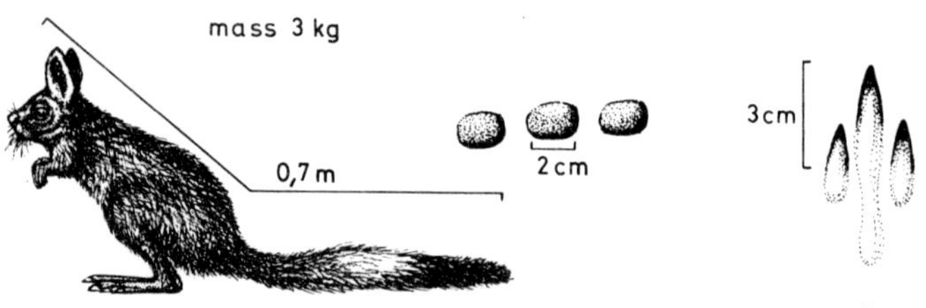

Fig. 76

Features The springhare rather resembles a hare both in shape and size but differs in that it has a long black-tipped tail, very much longer back legs than a hare, and much shorter ears. These animals have large eyes, fairly long soft fur, and long curved claws on the fore feet. The hind feet have hoof-like claws on each of the four hind toes, which are used for digging. When on the move they jump about on the hind legs like a kangaroo.

Habits Springhares live in burrows which they dig themselves and from which they emerge at night to feed. They prefer light sandy soils in which to make their burrows, and this largely determines their distribution. They are widespread in Zimbabwe, although absent from parts where the substrate is not suitable for digging, and they are not found in the Eastern Highlands.

The burrows are usually straight but may have a few turns. Often they have an entrance tunnel with the sand piled outside and an exit tunnel, dug from inside, with no sand pile outside. They do not form communal warrens, although some very suitable areas may be riddled with the individual burrows of pairs of springhares. Deserted burrows are often used for breeding or refuge purposes by pangolins, mongooses, polecats and other species.

Springhares are vegetarian, feeding mainly on the underground stems and rhizomes of grasses, but also raiding crops and often becoming a pest in this respect. Where they are unmolested they become quite tame. At Hwange Main Camp for example, one sometimes sees springhares hopping about between the chalets fairly late at night. Normally they are very alert and have keen hearing, sight and scent. When disturbed they make off in leaps and bounds with the tail held up over the back. This tail helps to maintain balance when the animal is leaping.

Breeding Single young are born in the burrows from about November to February.

Distribution They occur in southern Africa, including Angola and South West Africa, and extend north to Tanzania and Kenya.

Bibliography

ANSELL, W. F. H. *Mammals of Northern Rhodesia*, Government Printer, Lusaka, 1960

BARTLETT, DES *Nature's Paradise*, Collins, London, 1967

BERE, R. M. *The Wild Mammals of Uganda*, Longman, London, 1962

BERE, RENNIE *The African Elephant*, Arthur Baker, London, 1966

BURTON, M. *Dictionary of The World's Mammals*, Sphere Books Ltd, London, 1965

DORST, JEAN and DANDELOT, PIERRE *A Field Guide to the Larger Mammals of Africa*, Collins, London, 1970

EWER, R. F. *Ethology of Mammals*, Logos Press Ltd, 1968

EWER, R. F. *The Carnivores*, Weidenfeld & Nicholson, London, 1973

DE LA FUERTE, DR F. R. *Africa: Struggles for Survival in the Bush*, Orbis Publishing Ltd, London, 1970

HANZAK DR J., VESELOVSKY, DR Z. and STEPHEN, D. *Encyclopaedia of Animals*, Collins, London, 1968

KINGDON, JONATHAN *East African Mammals I*, Academic Press, 1971

Larousse Encyclopaedia of Animal Life, Paul Hamlyn, London, 1967

MABERLEY, CHARLES ASTLEY *The Game Animals of Southern Africa*, Nelson, London, 1963

MABERLEY, ASTLEY *Animals of Rhodesia*, Howard Timmins, Cape Town, 1963

MATTHEWS, L. HARRISON *The Life of Mammals*, Weidenfeld & Nicholson, London, 1969

MILLER, W. T. *Wildlife of Southern Africa*, Natal Witness Ltd

MITCHELL, B. L. and ANSELL, W. F. H. *Wildlife of Kafue and Luangwa*, Zambia Publishing Company Ltd, 1965

MORRIS, DESMOND *The Mammals*, Hodder & Stoughton, London, 1965

POTGIETER, D. J., DU PLESSIS, P. C. and SKAIFE, S. H. *Animal Life in Southern Africa*, Nasou Ltd, 1971

ROBERTS, AUSTIN *The Mammals of South Africa*, Published by the Trustees of The Mammals of South Africa Book Fund, South Africa, 1951

SMITHERS, DR REAY H. N. *The Mammals of Rhodesia, Zambia and Botswana*, Collins, London, 1966

SMITHERS, DR REAY H. N. *The Mammals of Botswana*, Museum Memoir No. 4, the Trustees of The National Museums and Monuments of Rhodesia, 1971

SMITHERS, DR REAY H. N. *Mammals. List of species known to occur in Rhodesia*, National Museums and Monuments of Rhodesia, 1973
SMITHERS, REAY H. N. and WILSON, V. J. *Check list and atlas of The Mammals of Zimbabwe*, Rhodesia National Museums and Monuments, Salisbury, Zimbabwe Rhodesia, 1979
SPINAGE, C. A. *The Book of the Giraffe*, Collins, London, 1968
The Living World of Animals, Reader's Digest Association, London, 1970
WALKER, ERNEST P. *Mammals of the World*, John Hopkins, London, 1964
YOUNG, J. Z. *The Life of Vertebrates*, O.U.P., London, 1962

The following journals and magazines were consulted:
African Wildlife, *Arnoldia*, *Koedoe*, *Puku*, *The Lammergeyer*, *Wild Rhodesia* and *Zoologica Africana*

Index

Plate references are shown in bold type

The Bundu Series

Birds of the Highveld, Peter Ginn, $5,95
Butterflies, Richard Cooper, $3,25
Aloes, Oliver West, $3,50
Some Well Known African Moths, Elliot Pinhey, $3,75
Snakes of Zimbabwe, Everard Cock and Donald Broadley, $6,95
Common Trees of the Highveld, Drummond and Palgrave, $12,95
Bird Safari, Peter Ginn, $11,25
Musi-oa-Tunya: A Handbook of Victoria Falls Region, ed. D. W. Phillipson, $7,50
Wild Flowers, Drummond and Plowes, $20,00
A Guide to the Rock Art, Cooke, $2,50
Aloes, $3,50

Bundu Books
Book 1: Trees, Flowers and Grasses, $7,75
Book 2: Birds, Insects and Snakes, $7,75
Book 3: Mammals, Reptiles and Bees, $7,75